All About
OLIVE OIL
Facts and Recipes

The World
of Olive Oil

ALMAZARA (Oil Press)   Engraving by J. Stadan, 17th century

THE VIRGIN GOLD OF THE OLIVE TREE

Manuel Piedrahita

1▲   2▲

A BRIEF HISTORY

The origins of the olive tree date back to around six thousand years ago in Asia Minor, in modern-day Turkey, at a time when wild olive trees were first cultivated for their fruit to obtain olive oil.

Olives were grown in Syria and Palestine long before the era of Christ. Numerous vestiges have been found, and literary references abound: in the Old Testament, for example, olives are mentioned in Jeremiah, Hosea, Joel, Deuteronomy, Ecclesiastes, Kings, Ezra and Ezekiel.

In the book of Judges, it is said that the olive did not wish to be the king of trees, so as to offer itself to man in the form of its olives:

"The trees went forth on a time to anoint a king over them; and they said unto the olive tree, Reign thou over us. But the olive tree said unto them, Should I leave my fatness, wherewith by me they honour God and man, and go to be promoted over the trees?"

In Leviticus we read: **"And the Lord spake unto Moses, saying, Command the children of Israel, that they bring unto thee pure oil olive beaten for the light, to cause the lamps to burn continually"**.

The book of Exodus also mentions **"unleavened bread, tempered with oil"**.

The olive, therefore, is a very old and much loved tree. It forms part of the culture of the remote civilisations which developed on both shores of the Mediterranean. Of all the peoples of the

1. Olives on the tree,
   ready to be harvested.
2. The Virgin Gold of the Olive Tree,
   freshly extracted.

3 ▲

sembly. It was decided to name the city after the divinity who created something useful for humanity. Whereas Neptune furiously struck a rock with his trident, producing a horse, Minerva proceeded to strike her lance into the ground, from where an olive tree sprung up. She was declared the victor, and once again the peaceful arts triumphed over war. The olive tree had beaten the horse.

The names for the tree in the various languages of the Mediterranean derive from the Cretan word *Elaiwa* and the Greek *Elaia*, later becoming the Latin *Oleum*. The Hebrew word *Zait*, when incorporated into Arabic, became *Az-Zait*, meaning "juice of the olive".

CULTIVATING THE OLIVE

Lucius Junius Moderatus Columella, the agricultural specialist of the first century AD, was born in Cádiz and died in Tarento. He considered the olive tree to be "*Olea prima arborum est*", the first among trees, and a symbol of wealth and status. Olives have been harvested to extract their oil from ancient times through to the present day. The Greeks and Romans considered it the main crop of "*Mare Nostrum*" and the people of the Mediterranean

area, olives were unknown only to the Assyrians and Babylonians.

The olive spread from the island of Cyprus to Anatolia, and from the island of Crete, where olives were grown as far back as 2500 BC, to Egypt. It was the Phoenicians who took the tree from the eastern Mediterranean to the west, by way of the Greek islands in the sixteenth century BC, and mainland Greece from

the fourteenth to twelfth centuries BC.

The olive tree plays a fundamental role in the mythological origins of Athens, the centre of Hellenic civilisation. Legend has it that following the argument between Minerva and Neptune over who would give their name to the city, it was agreed to obey the oracle, who proposed a solution from the people gathered in as-

3. Landscape of olive groves
   in southern Spain.

6

quickly began to find ways to improve their harvests and perfect the methods of oil extraction.

From the sixth century BC, a combination of invasions and trade saw the olive spread throughout the countries of the western Mediterranean. The Romans propagated the olive tree as a peaceful weapon in their conquests. Having been introduced in Spain during the maritime domination of the Phoenicians (1050 BC), olive farming developed with the arrival of Scipion (212 BC), during the Roman era. Olive groves were planted heavily in the Baetica area, where the climate was most favourable for the tree to thrive. The oil, which generally came from the towns of Seville, Córdoba and Écija, was shipped in ceramic amphorae throughout the Roman Empire, from Britannia to Egypt. In Rome the used amphorae were discarded at Mount Testaccio, where thousands have been found with their inscriptions intact.

From the earliest ages man learnt the science of farming and harvesting olives, a highly appreciated fruit for their oil, as a food and for many other uses. The inhabitants of both shores of the Mediterranean have made use of the olive's many advantages: the trimmed branches as cattle feed, olive pomace as a source of energy, and the residual vegetable water as fertiliser.

Baetica (modern-day Andalusia), was the first Roman province to supply olive oil. By the Middle Ages, the supremacy of olive oil from Spain, Italy and (to a lesser extent) Greece was undeniable.

But olives were not grown solely in the Mediterranean area; following the discovery of America in 1492, olive trees also spread to the New World. According to an incunabulum from 1530 housed in the Archivo de Indias in Seville, all ships headed for the Indies had to include at least a few olive seedlings amongst their cargo:

"Henceforth, all ship masters sailing for the Indies are to take with them on their vessel the amount of vine and olive plants which they see fit, so that no ship may sail without some amount on board."

It is no surprise, then, that olive trees spread to several countries in the Americas. Argentina has the greatest number of olive groves, covering 28,670 hectares. It is followed by the USA with 12,150, Mexico with 6,000, Peru with 5,605, Chile with 3,000, Uruguay with 900 and Brazil with 840.

In more recent times olive-growing has moved beyond the Mediterranean, and olive groves can now be found in places far removed from the trees ancient origins. Olives are grown as far afield as China (19,230 hectares), Australia (2,000 hectares) and South Africa (1,345 hectares).

It used to be said that "the Mediterranean ends where the olive does not grow". Today one might extend that to "wherever the sun allows it, the olive will grow and spread".

However, these areas are tiny when compared with the 7,955,340 hectares of olive groves which exist in the Mediterranean area. Spain heads the list with 2,127,000 hectares, followed by Italy with 1,141,350.

VARIETIES OF OLIVE AND DESIGNATIONS

Olives are grown practically all over Spain. The different varieties of olive are linked to their respective regions: *Gordal sevillano* (Seville), *Cornicabra* (Castile-La Mancha), *Picual* (Jaén), *Hojiblanca* (Málaga and Córdoba), *Picuda* or *Carrasqueña* (Córdoba), *Lechín* (Granada), *Arbequina* (Catalonia), *Empeltre* (Aragón), *Manzanilla cacereña* (Cáceres), *Verdial* (Huelva) and *Mallorquina* (Balearic Isles).

References exist of olive trees in the Canary Isles from 1403. Some botanists, mainly non-Spaniards, believe the Canary olive to be an indigenous variety, though it is more likely that it was taken to islands by Phoenician traders.

In Spain, the concept of DO or *Denominación de Origen* (Designation of Origin) is a mark of identity given to certain foods and drinks to guarantee their quality, and olive oil is no exception. Catalonia was the first area to have its designations of origin (Les Garrigues and Ciurana) approved by the Ministry of Agriculture and ratified by Brussels, in the late 1970s and early 1980s, followed by the DO Baena (Córdoba).

Since then the number has grown, with fifteen currently approved by the Ministry of Agriculture, Fisheries and Food (MAFF). The variety of olive, the microclimate, terrain, history and strict control from regulating councils are all fundamental elements for a DO application to be approved and then ratified by the EU, which covers virgin olive oils with a distinct personality in certain areas of the country.

The designations of origin for olive oil in Spain which are recognised by Brussels are:

Bajo Aragón (Teruel), **Baena** (Córdoba), **Les Garrigues** (Lérida), **Montes de Toledo** (Ciudad Real), **Priego de Córdoba** (Córdoba), **Sierra de Cazorla** (Jaén), **Sierra de Segura** (Jaén), **Sierra Mágina** (Jaén) and **Ciurana** (Tarragona).

Another six have been approved by the MAFF and are pending EU ratification. These are **Monterrubio** (Badajoz), **Gata-Hurdes** (Cáceres), **Montes de Granada** (Granada), **Oli Terra Alta** (Catalonia), **Sierra de Cádiz** (Cádiz) and **Mallorca** (Balearic Isles).

Other countries in or near the Mediterranean region (such as Portugal and the *Carrasquenha*) have the following varieties of olive:

Chemial from Algeria, French *Picholine*, *Kalamata* from Greece, *Sauri* from Israel, *Frantoio* from Italy, *Soury* from Lebanon, Moroccan *Picholine*, *Al-Zeity* from Syria, *Chetoul* from Tunisia, *Ayvalik* from Turkey, and *Obliga* from the former Yugoslavia.

Elsewhere, Argentina has *Arauco* and the USA has *Misión*.

PRODUCTION AND CONSUMPTION

World production of olive oil for the 2002/2003 season was 2,405,000 tons, slightly less than the 2001/2002 season, which yielded 2,825,500 tons.

4▼

4. Ripe olives.

Total production from the 15 EU countries was 1,863,500 tons.

Spain is the largest producer of olive oil in the world. Most Spanish oil comes from four regions, with the following (approximate) percentages: Andalusia 75%, Castile-La Mancha 14%, Extremadaura 6%, Catalonia 4%, and other regions 1%.

World-wide consumption of olive oil has grown steadily in recent years. The figure for the 2002/2003 season is around 1,574,500 tons, an increase of 14% over the previous season, an upward trend which has been notable for the last twenty years in EU countries.

Evolution of consumption per capita in the European Union

| | (kg/inhab./year) | |
	1982/83	2000/01
Germany	0.06	0.44
Belgium and Luxembourg	0.11	1.23
Denmark	0.02	0.47
Spain	9.43	14.48
France	0.49	1.55
Greece	20.81	25.45
Ireland	0.03	0.42
Italy	11.01	12.67
Holland	0.05	0.37
United Kingdom	0.03	0.57
Portugal	3.99	6.04
Austria	no data	0.51
Finland	no data	0.17
Sweden	no data	0.53

5▲

6▲

HARVESTING

The olive tree belongs to the Ligustrum botanical order, part of the Oleaceae family. Its fruit, the olive, is a more or less spherical drupe, the size of which depends on the variety. It is made up of the epicarp or skin, which is generally coloured when ripe, the pulp or mesocarp, which contains most of the oil, and the en-

5. Manual harvesting.
6. Vibrator shaking an olive tree.

7 ▲

docarp or stone, which is hard, long and pointed at the apex and which encloses a seed containing the embryo and food reserves. The fat from the stone can be considered seed oil; it is an expensive product, as it is highly prized in the cosmetics industry.

Harvesting olives, for both milling (to extract the oil) and table olives, is the most important job in an olive grove. It affects both the quantity and quality of the year's harvest, as well as affecting the following season. The ideal time for harvesting is when a diverse series of criteria are met.

The olive must have the maximum amount of oil, what is known as the fat yield. It must also be at its point of maximum quality. Harvesting for table olives begins in late August, when the olive is still very green and healthy. Olives for milling tend to be picked from mid-December, though this is often brought forward to early November, when the olive is not completely ripe

and is still on the tree. The oil obtained from these olives is of an unbeatable quality, the very finest olive juice.

Olives reach their maximum weight at the same time as their total pigmentation, when they are neither completely green nor completely black. From this point they begin to fall naturally from the tree. Any major delay from this moment on will affect the quality of the oil and can even lead to a drop in production for the following season. A late harvest, where olives are still on the tree, can affect the fruit's reserve of nutrients.

Prior to the harvest it is becoming more and more common to tend to the ground around the trees to prevent weeds and make it easier to collect the fallen olives. Mechanical sweeping devices are used for this task, with good economic results, although these olives do not make the best oil, and as such should be col-

▼8

lected separately from those taken straight from the tree. It is important to wash the olives, particularly those picked from the ground. Harvesting needs to be well organised to ensure a satisfactory yield in economic terms. Much progress has been made in this stage of the process, with ongoing innovation and some interesting solutions.

For harvesting olives from the tree a wooden pole around 3 or 4 metres long is still used, though a mechanical pole or beater which shakes the branches using a small motor is becoming increasingly commonplace. Another commonly used tool is the modern trunk shaker, which works by

7. Manual harvesting.
8. Mechanical harvester, sweeping up olives from the ground.

9▲

deño or "milking" the tree. The olives are picked by hand from the ground or from the tree by means of a stepladder, using a small device which removes the olives from the branch without harming them. The olives fall into baskets (known as *macacos* in some parts of Andalusia) which the pickers hang in front of them. In Catalonia, the pickers or *escarradors* pull the olives off the branches using combs called *sarpes* and *rasquetes*. In Aragón they use a type of staff known as a *gancho*.

In the Book of Agriculture (1513), Alonso de Herrera wrote the following: **"There are many ways of picking olives; but the**

gripping the trunk of the olive tree and exerting short, strong vibrations to make the olives fall off in one swift action, either onto matting or nets placed on the ground around the tree, or into a kind of inverted umbrella which fills with olives and is then twisted backwards to tip into a truck container. These systems were first used in California in 1946, and are now commonplace in Spain. Another mechanised method is to use bulky cyclone

machines, which produce a very strong gust of air, causing the olives to loosen and fall to the ground.

These systems are used on estates with a large production capacity and relatively flat land. Ideally the olives should be harvested from the tree (known as *vuelo*) and not from the ground. A more meticulous (and expensive) system is to pick by hand, a technique known as *or-*

9. A net full of olives being loaded onto a trailer to be taken to the press.
10. Hand-picked olives.
11. In areas with difficult access, mules are still used to transport the olives.

10▼

11▼

main method is by hand, with a step, without harming or bruising the olives, as it was an ancient precept that the olive must be neither bruised nor squeezed, because olives if squeezed by those picking them are greatly harmed, as they lose all that is new and tender (…) And if they cannot pick by hand, they are to shake the tree with a branch or staff, going with the grain and not against it, so as not to damage or break the branches, which can dry out and the tree will not recover for a long time."

All the mechanical systems which have been invented require the soil to be specially prepared. For this reason it is increasingly common not to till the ground around the trees, choosing instead to use herbicides throughout the year to keep the ground clean.

In days of old olives were cleaned where they were picked, using a sieve called a *cribón*. The cost that such a method would entail today has given way to a highly meticulous washing process at the mill, though the olives must still be transported without an excess of leaves or earth.

The transportation itself has also changed. The packs of mules loaded with sacks are a thing of the past, and the olives are now transported in trailers towed by tractors. It is important to avoid bumps and excessive loads, as crushing the olives will deteriorate the quality of the oil.

Olives picked from the ground are best transported separately to those picked from the tree. An oil obtained from the tree (*envero*) does not have the same quality as one extracted from olives which have spent several days on the ground. The fall may be natural or the result of winds or strong rain.

Usually the olives are transported in bulk, but the ideal method is in light plastic contain-

▼12

ers, as this allows for ventilation and prevents crushing.

12. Zuheros, a typical village in the middle of an important olive-growing area of Andalusia.

EXTRACTING THE OIL

The first mechanical elements to be used in agriculture were probably connected with the extraction of oil, which requires the following main operations:

Reception at the mill. The olives are tipped into the chutes to begin the cleaning process, and are then weighed electronically.

The milling itself, which breaks the skin of the olive and crushes the pulp.

Extracting the oil from the mass, either by pressing or by what are known as continuous systems.

Decanting, which separated the oil from the solid elements and added water, the residue (*alpechín*) of which is now called *alperujo* or two-phase pomace.

TRADITIONAL METHODS

The extraction of olive oil has gradually been perfected over the centuries. The traditional method using millstones is almost a thing of the past. The few that are left, at least in Spain, are increasingly becoming relics from a not too distant past. Hydraulic presses, which extract the oil by exerting pressure onto the mass of milled olives placed on a circular pulp mat (normally made from esparto or synthetic fibre), are also disappearing. This system revolutionised the oil industry, replacing beam presses and much earlier press-free extraction techniques.

In ancient times, olives were milled using a large stone or even one's feet. Stone rollers were developed in the Bronze Age, and were operated by hand or by means of a wooden framework. From this came the milling cylin-

der, which was operated either by man or by beast.

The beam press consisted of placing a stone over the crushed olive mass and waiting for the pressure to take effect. Later the technique was developed as actual machinery, by hang the stone from a beam.

In his **De re Rustica** and **De Arboribus**, written in 42 AD, Lucius Junius Moderatus Columella gives the first historic description of harvesting and milling olives:

13. A pressing plant
next to olive groves.

14▲

15▲

16▲

17▲

"As soon as the olives begin to change colour they are to be picked by hand in good weather, and placing mats or reeds underneath they are to be sieved and cleaned; once carefully cleaned, they are to be taken immediately to the mill, put in fresh baskets and placed under the mill, to be pressed for as short a time as possible. Then, having raised the presses, they must be milled thoroughly. After this, the first oil which has dripped into the bowl will be emptied by the cooper and transferred to the clay vessels made for this purpose. In the storage area there are three rows of pitchers, one for first-class oil, from the first pressing; another for the second, and the third row, for the third pressing; it is very important not to mix the second pressing, much less the third, with the first, as it is oil with a much better flavour which has been drained with lesser pressure from the mill."

18▲

19▲

20▲

21▲

▼22

Former systems
for obtaining olive oil.

14. Torsion system.
15. Beater pressure.
16. Roller pressure.
17. Treading method.
18. "Mola Olearia" mill.
19. "Trapetum" mill.
20. Wedge press.
21. Beam press.
22. Mill operated
    by moving water.

23▲

CONTINUOUS SYSTEMS

An essential part of oil extraction, whether the traditional methods described above or more advanced techniques are used, is to separate the oil from both the olive's residual water (*alpechín*) and the pomace of pulp and stone (*orujo*).

Traditional rollers and presses have now been replaced by mechanical hammer mills, used in what is known as continuous centrifugation, which takes place in two or three phases. This system of selective extraction was in-

23. Inside an oil press; with millstones and hydraulic presses, which although on the decline is still used in some places.

24▼

25▼

the few remaining presses which use traditional methods. In modern systems they have been replaced by small stainless-steel vats, where the oil is deposited for a short time to eliminate impurities before being sent to the much larger storage vats.

STONE-FREE EXTRACTION

This system is based on separating the stone completely and cleanly from the olive pulp,

▲26

vented by Miguel de Prado de Acapulco.

The paste obtained from the mechanical mills is partially diluted with hot water and sent to the stainless-steel horizontal centrifugal separator. Two nozzles, placed at different levels in the centrifuge, control the vegetation water and the oil, which passes into a vertical separator and is centrifuged for correct oil separation. The traditional decanting wells are a relic from the recent past, though they are still used in

24, 25 and 26. Continuous extraction systems, using mechanical mills, beaters and centrifuges.

27. The OroBaena plant, for stone-free extraction.

▼27

which is then sent straight to the crusher without being milled. The oil is extracted from the resulting mass without being altered in any way. The difference with regard to the continuous system described above is that there is no actual milling. The hammer mills used in continuous systems to crush the whole olive disappear. This advanced technology was successfully researched and developed in Italy and Spain. The OroBaena S.A.T. company from Baena (Córdoba) is the first business in Spain to fully use this system, which has become known as "twenty-first century milling".

Far from the oil losing any qualities when milled without the olive stone, this is in fact a more ecological oil.

STORAGE

The oil obtained at the mill needs to be stored for a certain time until it is sold or bottled. Recently extracted virgin oils have a series of properties that need to be maintained. They therefore require special storage conditions. The best deposits keep the temperature as stable as possible, preventing major changes. They are made from an inert material and shield the oil from air and light as far as possible.

Storage may be underground in concrete deposits, known as *trujales*, with vitrified tiles lining the interior. These deposits have replaced the huge earthenware storage containers which stood below ground level, with just the top few metres showing above the surface.

Stainless-steel deposits are now the norm, housed in acclimatised storage areas. It is important to maintain an average temperature of around 12º C all year round. Polyester deposits are also used; although easier to clean, they have transparent walls and require a coat of opaque paint on the outside before they can be used to store olive oil.

PACKAGING

The last stage in the olive oil production process, which began in the olive groves themselves, is the bottling or packing. Both co-operative and privately owned oil mills require a licence before their product can enter the market. Olive oil is an indispensable foodstuff, and its quality and health properties must be guaranteed, hence the care taken when bottling to ensure it is presented to consumers in the very best conditions. The packaging must allow the oil to keep. That said, the marketing factors involved in the presentation must also be considered; the label must be well designed, and consumers want to be able to appreciate the product they are buying. Metal, glass, PET and tetrabrik cartons are all used to package olive oil.

Virgin olive oil can be bottled *en rama* (unfiltered), maintaining all its properties, though filtered virgin olive oil also exists. This involves bringing out the oil's shine by eliminating moisture and preventing the formation of dregs. Glass bottles show these innocuous impurities most, yet they are neither harmful nor a symptom of deterioration, though people who do not understand oil can be put off by the appearance and doubt the quality of the product. To all this it must be added that olive oil can also be bought mixed with **refined** oil, which should not be confused with **filtered** oil.

Virgin olive oil known as *lampante* (the name comes from the fact that it was used in oil lamps) has defects originating from, among other things, a high acidity (over 3 grams per 100 grams), with the subsequent bad taste and smell. These oils are not fit for consumption, and their organoleptic conditions need to be corrected before they can be used as food. They therefore undergo a process called **refinement** or **rectification**, a process using physical methods resulting in a refined oil, with a very pale colour and little body. Refined oils have no taste or smell, and a very low acidity. They are strengthened with a virgin olive oil, and the resulting product is known simply as olive oil, previously (and erroneously) known as pure olive oil, which led to confusion.

The level of acidity in an olive oil does not mean the same as in wines. Used as a laboratory parameter for the amount of free fatty acids contained in a sample of oil, it does not mean that this particular sample of oil is stronger or smoother. Many consumers assume, through confusion or lack of knowledge, that a lower acidity makes for smoother oil, and a higher acidity a more intense flavour. There are virgin olive oils with only 0.2º and a very strong flavour. All low acidity means is that the oil comes from healthy olives, harvested when the olive is on the tree, and extracted in optimum conditions. In the case of olive oils, with a mix of virgin and refined oils, the low acidity is a re-

▲28

28. An old bodega with large storage vats, preserved but not in use.
29. A modern storage system, with conditioned stainless-steel vats.

sult of the refining or rectification process. It does not mean, therefore, that these oils are of a higher quality. For this reason it is no longer required for labels to indicate the acidity level.

▼29

REGULATIONS
FOR RATING OILS

The International Oil Council has established a Trade Standard for the physical, chemical and organoleptic characteristics of olive oils and olive-pomace oils, applicable to the international trade of these oils. The Trade Standard adopted on 25 June 2003 repeals the Standard of 8 November 2001. The following is an extract:

Olive oil is the oil obtained solely from the fruit of the olive tree (*Olea europaea*). It is marketed according to the following designations and definitions:

Olive oil: oils which are obtained from the fruit of the olive tree solely by mechanical or other physical means under conditions, particularly thermal conditions, that do not lead to deterioration of the oil, and which have not undergone any treatment other than washing, decanting, centrifugation and filtration.

Extra virgin olive oil: virgin olive oil which has a free acidity, expressed as oleic acid, of not more than 0.8 grams per 100 grams and the other characteristics of which correspond to those laid down for this category.

Virgin olive oil: virgin olive oil which has a free acidity, expressed as oleic acid, of not more than 2.0 grams per 100 grams and the other characteristics of which correspond to those laid down for this category.

Ordinary virgin olive oil: virgin olive oil which has a free acidity, expressed as oleic acid, of not more than 3.3 grams per 100 grams and the other characteristics of which correspond to those laid down for this category.

Lampante virgin olive oil: virgin olive oil which has a free acidity, expressed as oleic acid, of more than 3.3 grams per 100 grams. It is intended for refining for use for human consumption, or it is intended for technical use.

Refined olive oil: olive oil obtained from virgin olive oils using refining techniques which cause no modification to the initial glyceridic structure. It has a free acidity, expressed as oleic acid, of not more than 0.3 grams per 100 grams.

Olive oil: oil consisting of a blend of refined olive oil and virgin olive oils fit for consumption as they are. It has a free acidity, expressed as oleic acid, of not more than 1 gram per 100 grams.

30. Large open-air deposits, covered in insulating material.

OLIVE-POMACE OIL

As we have seen, the process of obtaining olive oil creates a by-product, the olive pomace, which contains most of the dry material from the olive (skin, pulp, seed and bits of stone) along with a certain amount of residual vegetation water. It also contains oil.

The quality of olive-pomace oil depends, first of all, on the characteristics of the pomace. The extraction system for this oil has steadily improved since the late nineteenth century. At first, organic solvents such as carbon sulphide were used, in factories known as *Fábricas Orujeras*.

The oils obtained were not fit for human consumption, and tended to be used to make soap. Later refining methods helped to obtain olive-pomace oils fit to be used as a foodstuff; the use of hexane solvents has made it possible to obtain much better olive-pomace oils.

The designations and definitions of olive-pomace oil, according to the Trade Standard described above, are as follows:

Olive-pomace oil: the oil obtained by treating olive pomace with solvents, or other physical procedures:

Crude olive-pomace oil: olive-pomace oil with the characteristics which correspond to those laid down for this category. It is intended for refining for use for human consumption, or it is intended for technical use.

Refined olive-pomace oil: the oil obtained from crude olive-pomace oil using refining techniques. It has a free acidity, expressed as oleic acid, of not more than 0.3 grams per 100 grams.

Olive-pomace oil: oil consisting of a blend of refined olive-pomace oil and virgin olive oils fit for consumption. It has a free acidity, expressed as oleic acid, of not more than 1 gram per 100 grams. In no case can this blend be designated "olive oil".

OIL TASTING

The quality of an olive oil is judged using a standardised international method established by the International Oil Council, which was approved in June 1987. Despite undergoing various revisions since then, the essential elements of the standard remain current for judging oils which are to be classified for their organoleptic characteristics or entered for an award.

A panel of tasters judging an oil is made up of 8 to 12 experts, all with a sound knowledge of oil types and quality, and who undergo an aptitude test before being selected.

The samples to be judged are labelled with a key by the panel chief. Each taster is given an opaque crystal glass (to hide the colour of the oil), into which 20 ml of oil are poured. The oil is heated to around 28 °C, the ideal temperature to release the oil's tastes and aromas. Each taster is isolated in a special booth with a profile sheet, where they note down the olfactory and taste sensations produced in the mouth by each sample of oil. Positive attributes include fruity, bitter and spicy, while negative elements include rancid, vinegary, fusty, acidic, musty, etc.

Having finished the tasting, the panel chief collects the profile sheets, which sometimes need to be repeated in the event of an incident or doubts about the judgement of a particular oil.

Finally, the panel chief uses a computer programme to calculate the evaluation of the virgin olive oils tasted.

Here are some of the terms used by tasters to define the virtues and defects of a sample of virgin olive oil:

Almond: A nutty, mainly almond, taste.

Fruity: Taste and aroma of green fruit, olive leaf. Can be strong or smooth.

Bitter: A bitter taste in the throat, can be more or less pleasant.

Sour: Astringent taste.

Fusty: A defective taste from when the olives have been kept for a long time in storage.

Wine: A taste that is reminiscent of wine or vinegar, of old olives.

Fragrant: A clean, fresh taste, richly aromatic.

Grassy: A taste of freshly cut grass.

Metallic: A taste of metal, due to the olives entering into contact with metal surfaces.

Earthy: A taste of earth, from olives with soil which were not properly washed.

OLIVE OIL AND HEALTH

It has been scientifically proven that olive oil contains a series of elements which are highly beneficial to a large part of the human body. This modern view was also held in ancient times. Hippocrates prescribed olive oil for ulcers and cholera, and as an ointment for muscular pain. Pliny the Elder (first century AD) wrote a treaty on the curative properties of the olive tree and the oil obtained from its fruit: when mixed with honey it heals wounds; it can be used in drops to treat eye diseases; the roots of the olive tree, when crushed and added to honey, cure bronchial diseases. He also advocated drinking olive-leaf infusions as an excellent cleansing medicine.

The therapeutic properties of olives themselves are related to their chemical structure. Olive oil has a predominance of mono-unsaturated fatty acids, mainly oleic acid. Animal fats are made up of polyunsaturated acids, and are much less stable than mono-unsaturated acids against the process of oxidation.

The chemical make-up of olive oil is particularly interesting, not just for its composition of acids but also for its lesser elements, in particular antioxidants (tocopherol, phenolic compounds and carotenoids), of which it contains large amounts. This richness in antioxidants is perhaps due to the fact that the olive is a fruit exposed to the air and must defend itself from the oxygen. Unlike seeds (such as sunflowers), therefore, olives contain a greater amount of antioxidant substances, which are present in the oil.

A diet rich in monounsaturated fatty acids based on antioxidant components (vitamin E) acts as a defence mechanism for the human organism which, by law of nature, is constantly growing old. Olive oil is ideal for preventing phenomena which lead to ageing, due to the high content of anti-oxidants and the very low content of saturated fatty acids. Olive oil has a favourable effect on bone mineralisation. It is indispensable during the growing age, but also as an adult to slow the loss of calcium, which increases with age.

A diet with olive oil is necessary for both children and adolescents. A diet poor in olive oil can delay growth. Studies exist which have detected alteration in the brain's structural lipids in groups of children treated with saturated fats and sunflower oil, but not in those given olive oil.

Arteriosclerosis is one of the most common diseases in industrialised countries. It is a veritable plague and the main cause of mortality, due not only to genetic predisposition but also to lifestyle: stress, an inadequate diet and the abusive consumption of alcohol and tobacco. The consequences are high blood pressure and cardiovascular diseases in general.

Cholesterol is a lipid abundant in animal tissue. A diet rich in animal fats helps to increase the level of cholesterol in the plasma (LDL). The opposite occurs with a diet featuring olive oil as a basic ingredient, rich in monounsaturated fats, which also helps to raise levels of "good" cholesterol (HDL). The studies carried out by Professor Grande Covian and Professor Keys have shown a higher incidence of heart diseases in Finnish and North American people, with a low intake of olive oil, than in people from the Mediterranean area where olive oil is a common element of the daily diet.

Research in both Europe and the USA has confirmed the protective effect of olive oil against breast cancer, particularly in menopausal women. This protection may be related to monounsaturated fatty acids.

The reason given by new consumers of olive oil, from non-producing countries with diets not based on olive oil, is that it is a product with scientifically proven beneficial effects on health.

OLIVE OIL AND THE MEDITERRANEAN DIET

The Mediterranean diet or cuisine, which is based fundamentally on olive oil, and with a predominantly vegetable content (fruit, vegetables, pulses), is the most suitable for preventing all kinds of diseases. As Professor Francisco Mataix Verdú puts it, "normally we do not reflect that when we eat, not only do we satisfy the physiological need of hunger and the pleasing aspect of a tasty dish, we are also supplying the organism with the basic pieces so that, suitably digested and metabolised, they contribute towards good health and, in a wider sense, to a long life".

The great chefs of the world have praised olive oil for use in frying, to dress salads and, above all, to condiment all kinds of dishes from the simple to the sophisticated, as was seen in the Second International Gastronomic Summit held in Madrid in January 2004. The exhibition by three young chefs titled "The Thousand and One Uses of Olive Oil" was a total success. Olive oil is being used more and more by the best chefs (as well as cooks in more modest restaurants) to prepare their dishes. The most avant-garde cuisine is using more olive oil, and whereas before famous chefs would wonder "what dish can I use olive oil in?" (as butter was much more common), they might now ask "what don't I use it in?".

As was made clear in the International Summit, olive oil confers flavours and aromas to food, apart from its use at high temperature. Haute cuisine holds olive oil in high regard in its new technique of frying/cooking. Olive oil should always be used in pasta recipes, and not just because olive oil is produced and consumed in Italy. Spaghetti, for example, is much smoother when a little virgin olive oil is added to the boiling water.

A good salad, properly dressed, is an ideal accompaniment to a pasta dish. A raw extra virgin oil with all its unfiltered properties enhances vegetables, as well as the traditional *gazpacho*, and the *salmorejo* of Córdoba or *porra* of Antequera, which was also exhibited in the International Summit. And let us not forget a slice of crunchy bread soaked in a good raw oil, the epitome of a healthy breakfast for the heart, promoted in schools in Asturias by Dr Jesús Bernardo.

The food critic José Carlos Capel says that olive oil should be used in both haute cuisine and popular cooking, and not just for frying or to dress salads. In stews and sautés, as with meat and fish, the aroma and flavour of olive oil complements the ingredients used. In roasts, olive oil is most suitable for its stability and adaptability to high temperatures. The same can be said of grilled, pan-fried and barbecued foods. And the best mayonnaise is made with a fruity virgin olive oil.

Olive oil is also beginning to replace butter in artisan confectionery, albeit slowly. Traditional lard cakes are now made in two batches: one with pork lard and another with olive oil. Homemade sponges can be made perfectly well with a good virgin olive oil instead of the butter stated in the recipe.

The art of cooking needs to be applied well when using the wide variety of virgin olive oils that exist on the market. An ideal situation is to have several oils in the kitchen, provided one knows how to judge their organoleptic qualities. There are oils which are more or less fruity; there are those which are smooth, and others with more body. Some can be used raw, and others in stews or for frying. That said, the general rule is that if you are in the habit of using a good extra virgin olive oil, one which is fruity, smooth, not too bitter and not too spicy in the throat, yet has the aroma of an olive grove, it can be used for all kinds of dishes. It is like drinking a good red wine, which will go well with fish and meat, regardless of convention.

FRYING WITH OLIVE OIL

Frying is the most suitable way to make food agreeable to the palate. It is also the oldest and most popular form of cooking throughout the Mediterranean. This tradition is linked to a culture or lifestyle which goes hand in hand with olive growing. Olive oil has no competition when it comes to being heated and used for frying. Compared with other liquid fats, it is the most resistant to oxidative deterioration. Frying with olive oil allows the food to withstand very high temperatures; it can reach 100 ºC and remain constant until the water contained in the food has evaporated.

One of the simplest ways of checking if the oil is ready for frying is to add a few pieces of bread to the pan: if the bread sinks to the bottom and remains there, the oil is too cold, at around 150 °C. If the bread rises slowly to the surface, the oil is ready to fry delicate foods such as vegetables and slices of bread, at a temperature between 160 °C and 165 °C. If the bread rises immediately, then the oil is ready to fry at high temperatures, around 170 °C to 175 °C. And if the bread does not sink at all and burns, the oil is too hot, at around 180 °C to 190 °C.

Hot olive oil acts very quickly, and as such fried foods lose less of their nutritional value than during other culinary processes. Studies by Professor Varela have shown that foods fried at a high temperature in olive oil do not lose their digestibility.

The increased stability of olive oil means that it can be used for frying more times than other vegetable fats. It is extremely stable at high temperatures, such as when frying several batches of potatoes. It forms a crust on the outside of the food, such as breaded fish and meat, giving improved taste and texture.

Habits when frying food are very similar, though there are differences. In Spain and Italy food is generally floured before frying; in France ingredients are dipped in milk and egg, then rolled in flour; in England they are coated in egg and breadcrumbs; in Japan, where food is also fried, it is dipped in a mixture of flour and water; and in China food is fried at a very high temperature using only a small amount of oil.

However, all this depends on knowing how to fry food, which is an uncommon skill. The olive oil should not be blamed when the food is greasy, lacks the right texture or is raw on the inside. With a good olive oil at the right temperature, fried food comes out perfect. The result is food which is good for the heart and gastronomically unbeatable.

It is advisable to filter oil after frying. Remains of food can dirty the oil and alter its properties. Some foods leave more residue than others. Fish, for example, leaves a very definite flavour in the oil. Potatoes damage the oil very little, and as such the oil can be used more than once. The general rule is to fry five or six times with the same oil, but always for the same type of food; when cooking a different kind, fresh oil should be used.

THE OLIVE TREE IN LITERATURE

Since ancient times the olive tree has been the subject of praise and emotion in Mediterranean literature. This humble tree offers up its fruit so men can feed themselves with the oil extracted. Olive trees create a landscape where the imagination can run free with poems and poetic prose. The following are just a few excerpts from the countless examples which can be found in libraries all over the world:

"Now there is in Ithaca an old haven, which lies between two points that break the line of the sea and shut the har-bour in. These shelter it from the storms of wind and sea that rage outside (…) At the head of this harbour there is a large olive tree…"**
(Homer in The Iliad)

"How can I explain that even 100 times dead I shall miss my land, Córdoba; how to explain that my only wish, now that I am dying, is to know I am to be buried in the shade of an olive tree, under living earth, listening to the song of the muezzin, the gurgling water of envy…"
(Averroes)

"Allah is the light of the heavens and the earth; a likeness of His light is as a niche in which is a lamp, the lamp is in a glass, and the glass is as it were a brightly shining star, lit from a blessed olive tree, the oil whereof almost gives light though fire touch it not - light upon light…"
(The Koran)

In her **"Tribute to Oil"**, Gabriela Mistral describes it as **"Neither sweet nor savoury, like wisdom itself"**, adding later: **"Oil, slower than a tear, more paused than blood"**.

Andalusia has long red roads. Córdoba, green olive groves…
(Federico García Lorca)

Andalusians of Jaén, olive-pickers proud, tell me from the soul: Who, who raised the olive trees?
(Miguel Hernández)

Solitary olive tree
By the fountain, far from
the grove
hospitable olive tree.
(Antonio Machado)

Not only sings the wine,
for oil also sings…
(Pablo Neruda)

SYMBOL OF PEACE

The olive is a mythological tree rich in symbolism. It has existed since ancient times, symbolising immortality and peace. The dove with the olive branch in its peak remains a powerful symbol of peace; the flood did not affect the olive, and Noah deemed it the tree of reconciliation.

The dove with the olive branch has been used extensively as a symbol on coins over the centuries, and Greek coins have been found featuring the owl and the olive tree as tributes to Athena. A medal commemorating the Spanish Constitution of 1812, in Cádiz, bears the image of the goddess Athena.

Another famous image is the dove of peace by Picasso.

In The Aeneid, Virgil tells how Aeneas navigates the Tiber until arriving at the city where King Evander awaits. His son, Pallas, asks Aeneas: "Who are you? Do you bring war or peace?", and Aeneas shows him an olive branch.

The entrance of Jesus in Jerusalem is described in the New Testament with a clear allusion to the tree of peace: "And a very great multitude spread their garments in the way; others cut down branches from the trees, and strawed them in the way".

Olive branches are blessed on Palm Sunday as a religious symbol. The olive tree is also linked to the last week of Christ's life, to the Passion. Legend has it that the cross on which Jesus was crucified was made from olive wood. The Garden of Olives, where Jesus prayed before being arrested, is called Gethsemane, which means "oil press". Thousand-year old olives can still be seen in that place.

BY WAY OF AN EPILOGUE

I vividly remember a time in my childhood which might just serve as an epilogue for this book. With retrospective melancholy I see my maternal grandmother sat at the table, eating an orange split into pieces and dribbled in olive oil winding its way around the white plate from la Cartuja in Seville and on which my grandfather soaked a piece of rustic bread. In my memory I can hear him clearly...

"This is a delicacy enjoyed by the king of England himself."

From my current perspective I know not if that comment was true or if my uncle was merely trying to instil in me, as a child, the habit of such good eating; with the reference to the British Empire, his mention of royalty was enough to emphasise this gastronomic delight - the vitamins of the orange, the oil and the bread; a delicacy from the gods of Greek mythology and Roman emperors...

Is there anything more natural, more rural (and thus more noble), than an orange, an olive tree and an ear of wheat? Three essential pillars of the gastronomic culinary of the Mediterranean, three traditional ingredients of a healthy diet.

The miller's lunch, the usual midday meal for the oil press workers ("*cagarraches*"), is another basic element of the traditional gastronomy in olive-growing areas. The night shift would end around noon, and the millers arriving and leaving at around this time would gather together in the main storage cellar and tuck in to their grub.

As a child I was present at some of these millers' meals, and I remember a rustic loaf of bread toasted in the mill's oven being hung from a string and submerged into the depths of a large jar of freshly pressed virgin olive oil. Once completely soaked it was lifted back up and placed in a bowl along with the juice of a pomegranate or an orange. This fine delicacy was known as *remojon*.

I would recommend this nineteenth-century tradition to the restaurants of the twenty-first: the bread, sprinkled with sugar and cinnamon and then soaked in a mixture of virgin olive oil and orange or pomegranate juice, is an exquisite delicacy.

The essential element of the millers' lunch was the hot bread dribbled with oil and spread with garlic, tomato and orange. It would be the perfect aperitif for a meal where I would serve, first of all, the excellent traditional Córdoba dish of *salmorejo*, made with virgin olive oil and wine vinegar; smooth and creamy, it is a true delight to the taste buds. The virgin olive oil acts as a nexus for the tomato, bread, garlic and other ingredients.

(I "exported" this dish to Germany, and still remember with glee how those folks from the Rhineland, used to sausages and goose fat, insisted on this fine dish, so delicate, so nutritious, so healthy...)

Let us continue with a few prawns, not cooked but fried, with skill and a good olive oil, previously coated in flour and free-range egg. They make the perfect excuse to serve a good mayonnaise, which when prepared with extra virgin olive oil makes an indispensable sauce for the most demanding gastronomy. Sadly, many cooks at home use other liquid fats (I use the word fat rather than oil or *aceite*, as the word comes from *aceituna*, the Spanish for olive...) thinking that this will make a smoother mayonnaise. What a monumental error! We are confusing smooth with aseptic. Those sauces either taste of nothing at all, or are too strong to enjoy.

Industrial mayonnaise tastes of chemical products imitating a natural flavour. And the natural flavour is the slight bitterness of the oil wrapped in the pleasing acidity of a good lemon. A free-range egg and a sprinkle of sea salt will do the rest.

And what horror, what tremendous horror! When eggs are fried or a Spanish omelette is made using those liquid fats that leave a strange urban taste on such popular, traditional dishes. I yearn for fried eggs and pan-fried spuds, *patatas a lo pobre*, poor-man's potatoes; poor they may be, yet they are rich in olive oil. A few pieces of fried garlic over the golden egg yolk, with oil spreading out over the plate, is a culinary tradition based on the goodness of the olive oil.

Let us now try some wedding meatballs, as they are known. Personally I have a weakness for these subtle, delicate meatballs, floating in a lovingly made broth. Every time I pass a hamburger restaurant (I pass but do not enter), I remember those nuptial, virginal meatballs, which originated in the village of Luque, in the province of Córdoba. The bride's friends would carefully prepare this dish the morning after the wedding night, and would place it at the entrance of the bedroom, so that when the newlyweds awoke they could regain their strength.

To finish off sweetly, I also miss the *pestiños* and *flores de sartén* of my childhood: flour, sugar, a touch of wine and sesame seeds, made into a dough and fried with all the skill of frying well in olive oil. And I cannot forget the mystical touch of the nuns in the convent, with their *pestiños* prepared with such modest restraint between prayers and religious songs. Juan Valera, the nineteenth-century writer born in Cabra and native of Doña Mencía, sings his finest praises to these culinary traditions, so intrinsically linked to festivals and celebrations.

A good virgin olive oil, then, is an integral part of a traditional gastronomic culture, that of the Mediterranean diet, which I would sum up in three words:

Simple, tasty and healthy.

Manuel Piedrahita works as a journalist. He was correspondent for various Spanish newspapers, both in London and, years later, in Germany as a correspondent for Spanish Public Television (TVE).

*He has published **Tierra de Olivos** in collaboration with photographer Alberto Schommer, and **Mi olivo, tu olivo, nuestro olivo**; an anthology of articles written for the Diario Córdoba newspaper and other media outlets.*

Manuel Piedrahita is president of the Guild of Friends of the Olive of Baena, director of the magazine Tierra de Olivos published by the DO Baena Regulating Council, and a founding member of the company OroBaena, S.A.T.

Recipes
and Olive Oil

AJOBLANCO
WHITE GAZPACHO SOUP

Ingredients (serves four)

- 200 g (7 oz) peeled almonds
- 200 g (7 oz) bread crumbs
- 4 cloves garlic
- 150 ml (¼ pint) olive oil
- 1 l (2 pints) water
- Vinegar
- Salt

Preparation

Use a blender to mix the almonds, garlic and bread (soaked in milk) to form a paste. Add the olive oil slowly, while blending, to form a mix the consistency of mayonnaise. Stir in the water, along with salt and vinegar.

Check again for salt and vinegar before storing in the refrigerator (to serve cold).

Can be served with grapes, small pieces of fried bread and apple.

CREMA DE CHAMPIÑONES
CREAM OF MUSHROOMS SOUP

Ingredients (serves four)

- 300 g (10 oz) mushrooms
- 100 ml (3¹/₂ oz) cream
- 50 g (2 oz) grated cheese
- 500 ml (1 pint) milk
- 500 ml (1 pint) stock
- 1 onion
- Ground white pepper
- 3 tbsp flour
- 200 ml (¹/₃ pint) olive oil
- Salt

Preparation

Clean and slice the mushrooms. Finely chop the onion and sauté in olive oil, and before they brown add the mushrooms. Pour in a cup of stock (stock cubes can be used) and cook on a low heat for ten minutes.

Meanwhile prepare a béchamel sauce: heat a cupful of olive oil in a pan, add three spoonfuls of flour and stir well, then slowly add the milk, stirring constantly to prevent lumps. After ten minutes add salt and the mushrooms. Stir well then blend, adding more stock if needed, to form a smooth texture before adding the cream.

Serve hot, sprinkled with the grated cheese and white pepper.

CREMA DE SALMÓN
CREAM OF SALMON SOUP

Ingredients (serves four)

- 500 g (1 lb) salmon
- 2 leeks
- 1 onion
- 2 carrots

- 3 tomatoes
- 500 ml (1 pint) cream
- 1 tsp paprika
- Ground white pepper

- 150 ml (1/4 pint) olive oil
- Salt

Preparation

Finely chop the onion, carrots and leeks, and sauté in olive oil on a low heat so that they do not brown. After five minutes add the peeled and chopped tomato, and stir well. Remove the skin and bones from the salmon, chop into small pieces and add to the pan. Stir in the cream, a spoonful of paprika, and a pinch of salt and pepper, and leave to cook for around ten minutes.

After this time, liquefy with the blender and pass through a sieve, to ensure a smooth cream.

Check for salt and pepper before serving hot.

CREMA DE SOPA DE AJO
CREAM OF GARLIC SOUP

Ingredients (serves four)

- 250 g (9 oz) thinly sliced stale bread
- 4 cloves garlic
- 4 tsp paprika
- 1 tsp chilli powder
- 100 ml (7 tbsp) olive oil
- Salt

Preparation

Chop the garlic and gently fry in the olive oil (not too hot). When they begin to colour add the paprika and chilli and the bread, stirring so that the bread soaks up some of the oil. Cover with water and cook for 10 to 15 minutes, checking for salt. Blend the mixture to combine all the ingredients then sieve or pass through a colander to ensure the cream is as smooth as possible.

Serve hot.

GAZPACHO
COLD TOMATO SOUP

Ingredients (serves four)

- 750 g (1 3/4 lb) ripe tomatoes
- 250 g (9 oz) stale bread
- 1 green pepper
- 1 cucumber
- 1 clove garlic
- Vinegar
- 200 ml (1/3 pint) olive oil
- Salt

Preparation

Peel and chop the tomatoes and cucumber, slice the pepper, peel and halve the garlic and break up the bread. Place all these ingredients in a blender and mix along with the oil, a tablespoon of vinegar and a teaspoon of salt.

Blend to form a smooth cream, then add 500 ml (just under a pint) of water. Mix well and check for vinegar and salt, adding more if needed (or a little more water).

Place in the refrigerator for a few minutes, to be served cold.

Stir well before serving. Accompany with small pieces of tomato, cucumber, croutons and even hardboiled egg on the side, to be added to the soup according to taste.

SOPA DE MARISCOS
SEAFOOD SOUP

Ingredients (serves four)

- 1 kg (2 lb) mussels
- 500 g (1 lb) monkfish
- 350 g (11 oz) clams
- 1 onion

- 2 tomatoes
- 2 cloves garlic
- 1 tablespoon paprika
- 6 sprigs parsley

- 4 tbsp breadcrumbs
- 100 ml (7 tbsp) olive oil
- Salt

Preparation

First clean the mussel shells, then place in a pan, cover with water and cook until they open. Allow to cool a little before removing from the shells, then chop and put to one side (discard the shells). Sieve the cooking water and put to one side.

Finely chop the onion and garlic, and sauté in a frying pan with olive oil. Peel and chop the tomato, and add to the pan when the onion begins to brown, along with the chopped parsley. Cook for four or five minutes before removing from the heat and adding the paprika.

Remove the skin and bones from the monkfish and put to one side. Chop the fish into pieces (not too large), and peel the raw prawns (keep the heads and shells).

Bring a litre and a half (2.5 pints) of water to the boil, along with the mussels water, the monkfish bones and the prawn heads and shells. Remove from the heat after a few minutes and sieve. Bring this sieved stock to the boil again and add the monkfish pieces. Cook for ten minutes before adding the prawns, clams, mussels and onion sauté. For a slightly thicker soup add three or four spoonfuls of breadcrumbs. Check for salt and leave to cook for a further six or seven minutes before serving.

SOPA DE TOMATE
TOMATO SOUP

Ingredients (serves four)

- 750 g (1 3/4 lb) ripe tomatoes
- 2 cups thin slices stale bread
- 3 green peppers
- 1 onion
- 2 cloves garlic
- 1/2 tsp fresh mint
- 4 eggs (optional)
- 100 ml (7 tbsp) olive oil
- Salt

Preparation

Peel and chop the tomatoes. Chop the garlic, onion and peppers.

Cover the bottom of a casserole dish (preferably earthenware) with olive oil and sauté the onion, pepper and garlic until they begin to brown, and then add the tomato.

When the vegetables are well cooked, cover with water, season and simmer for ten minutes on a low heat. Now add the two cupfuls of bread and the mint. Leave to cook for five more minutes.

Can be served with poached egg.

SOPA JULIANA
JULIENNE SOUP

Ingredients (serves four)

- 2 leeks
- 150 g (5 oz) cabbage
- 200 g (7 oz) cauliflower
- 2 medium potatoes
- 1 onion
- 4 sprigs parsley
- 1 carrot
- 2 cloves garlic
- 75 ml (5 tbsp) olive oil
- Salt

Preparation

Wash the vegetables and chop in julienne. Bring water to the boil and add the vegetables, oil and salt, and cook until almost tender. Dice the potatoes and add to the pan, then cook for a further five minutes until all the vegetables are ready.

Meanwhile, finely chop two cloves of garlic and the parsley and sauté in olive oil until they begin to brown, then add to the soup and simmer for two more minutes. Check for salt and serve.

ALCACHOFAS RELLENAS DE ANCHOAS
ARTICHOKES STUFFED WITH ANCHOVIES

Ingredients (serves four)

- 8 artichokes
- 1 lemon
- 1 onion
- 3 tomatoes

- 16 anchovies in oil
- 50 g (2 oz) breadcrumbs
- 75 ml (5 tbsp) olive oil
- Salt

Préparation

Remove the harder outer leaves of the artichokes and leave a stalk of around 3 cm (1 inch). Use a knife to empty out the middle, forming little bowls. Cook for around half an hour in plenty of boiling salted water, with the juice of the lemon to prevent discoloration. Once cooked, drain well and place in an ovenproof dish.

Meanwhile, finely chop the onion and fry with olive oil until tender, then add the peeled chopped tomato and cook for five minutes. Lightly season and add the anchovies and chopped artichoke stems.

Stuff the artichokes with this sauce, sprinkle with the breadcrumbs and place in the oven at 180° C (360° F) for five minutes to grill.

ALUBIAS CON ACELGAS
HARICOT BEANS WITH CHARD

Ingredients (serves four)

- 500 g (1 lb) haricot beans
- 750 g (1 ³/₄ lb) chard
- 2 chorizo sausages
- 4 cloves garlic
- 3 tomatoes
- 10 raw almonds
- Paprika
- 1 dried red pepper
- 100 ml (7 tbsp) olive oil
- Salt

Preparation

Soak the beans and pepper in water overnight.

Cook the beans in salted water with two spoonfuls of olive oil, simmering for an hour until tender (the time will depend on the type of beans).

Meanwhile, cook the chard for ten minutes in salted water, then drain thoroughly, chop and put to one side.

Chop the garlic and almonds and fry in olive oil until brown, then crush in a mortar and put to one side.

Peel and chop the tomatoes, and lightly fry along with the sliced chorizo. When done add a spoonful of paprika and remove from the heat.

Add the sauté, the chard, the garlic with almonds and the chopped pepper to the beans. Cook for a further twenty minutes, seasoning to taste before serving.

ALUBIAS CON ALMEJAS
HARICOT BEANS WITH CLAMS

Ingredients (serves four)

- 500 g (1 lb) haricot beans
- 500 g (1 lb) clams
- 500 ml (1 pt) fish stock
- 1 onion

- 1 bay leaf
- 5 sprigs parsley
- 1 tablespoon flour
- 2 cloves garlic

- 1 glass white wine
- 100 ml (7 tbsp) olive oil
- Salt

Preparation

Leave the beans to soak in cold water overnight.

The next day, cook the beans in fresh cold water, adding the chopped onion, the bay leaf and a little olive oil when the water boils. Leave to simmer for three hours (this will depend on the type of bean).

Finely chop the garlic and fry in olive oil until brown, then add the chopped parsley, a spoonful of flour, the white wine and the fish stock, and boil for two minutes before adding the carefully washed clams. When their shells open, add the whole mix to the cooked beans. Add salt and cook everything together for five minutes, shaking the pan to make sure the clams and beans are thoroughly mixed together.

ALUBIAS CON ARROZ
HARICOT BEANS WITH RICE

Ingredients (serves four)

- 300 g (10 oz) haricot beans
- 200 g (7 oz) rice
- 150 g (5 oz) pork fat
- 150 g (5 oz) pork lean

- 2 green peppers
- 4 cloves garlic
- 1 potato
- 3 tomatoes

- Saffron
- 200 ml ($^1/_3$ pint) olive oil
- Salt

Preparation

Soak the beans in water overnight.

Cover the beans with water in a pan, along with two tablespoons of olive oil and salt. Cook for around two hours, depending on the type of beans (add more cold water if needed). Halfway through this time, add a few sprigs of saffron.

Meanwhile, peel and dice the potatoes, slice the garlic and fry gently in olive oil so the potatoes are soft. Remove from the pan, mash with a fork and put to one side.

Use the same oil to fry the green peppers and the pork fat and lean (all chopped); when they are cooked add the potato and garlic mixture.

When the beans are soft, add them to the mixture.

Bring to the boil, add the rice, check for salt and cook for fifteen minutes, adding more cold water if needed, to produce a stew with a slight broth.

ALUBIAS CON POLLO
HARICOT BEANS WITH CHICKEN

Ingredients (serves four)

- 500 g (1 lb) haricot beans
- Half a chicken, in pieces
- 2 tomatoes
- 2 onions

- 1 leek
- 2 carrots
- 1 clove garlic
- 1 sachet saffron

- 2 glasses white wine
- 150 ml ($^1/_4$ pint) olive oil
- Salt

Preparation

Place the beans in cold water to soak overnight.

Finely chop an onion, a carrot, a tomato and the leek, place in a pan with the rinsed beans, olive oil and salt, and cover with water. Bring to the boil and then simmer on a low heat until the beans are soft (the time will depend on the type of beans). Add a little saffron halfway through the cooking process.

While the beans are cooking, prepare the chicken. Clean it well and cut into pieces, rub with salt and crushed garlic, and dress with a little olive oil and white wine. Brown the chicken pieces in plenty of hot olive oil, then remove and place in a new pan. Use the oil from the chicken to sauté the other chopped onion and carrot, and after a few minutes add the other peeled chopped tomato. Add this mixture to the chicken along with the white wine and cook for around fifty minutes or until the chicken is tender and the meat comes off the bone easily. Finally, add all this to the beans and cook for a few more minutes, shaking the pan several times to mix all the ingredients well, and check for salt.

If the beans need any more liquid adding at any point, always use cold water.

BERENJENAS RELLENAS DE PISTO CON CARNE
AUBERGINES STUFFED WITH RATATOUILLE AND BEEF

Ingredients (serves four)

- 2 aubergines
- 150 g (5 oz) minced beef
- 3 rashers bacon
- 1 onion
- 1 green pepper

- $1/2$ courgette
- 2 tomatoes
- 100 g ($3^1/2$ oz) wild mushrooms
- 150 ml ($1/4$ pint) olive oil
- Salt

Preparation

Slice the aubergines in half, then use a knife to empty the insides.

Chop the onion, green pepper, courgette and aubergine flesh and fry gently in a casserole dish with olive oil. Peel and chop the tomatoes and add to the sauté when the vegetables are soft. Season with salt and leave to cook for a few minutes on a low heat.

Cut the bacon into strips and season the mince, then sauté in olive oil.

Season the aubergine skins and rub them in olive oil, then place them in an oven preheated to 180° C (360° F) for two or three minutes.

Meanwhile, slice the wild mushrooms into strips and sauté in olive oil.

Mix the vegetables with the mince and the bacon and stuff the aubergine skins, making sure everything is hot. Lay the wild mushrooms over the top and serve.

BUÑUELOS DE ALCACHOFAS
ARTICHOKE FRITTERS

Ingredients (serves four)

- 12 artichokes
- 200 g (7 oz) flour
- 75 ml (5 tbsp) beer
- 1 tsp baking powder
- 2 cloves garlic
- 1 lemon
- 200 ml ($1/3$ pint) olive oil
- Salt

Preparation

Prepare the batter by mixing the flour, baking powder and salt, then pouring in the beer to form a thick cream. Finely chop or crush the garlic and add to the mix, then leave to sit for half an hour.

Meanwhile, prepare the artichokes: cut the stems and remove the outer leaves, so that just the heart of the artichoke, then cook in plenty of boiling salted water with lemon juice to prevent discoloration. Cook for around half an hour until they are tender and can be easily pierced with a needle.

Coat each artichoke in the batter and fry in plenty of olive oil until brown.

GARBANZOS A LA RIOJANA
LA RIOJA-STYLE CHICKPEAS

Ingredients (serves four)

- 500 g (1 lb) chickpeas
- 100 g (3½ oz) cured ham
- 100 g (3½ oz) pork fat
- 1 beef bone
- 1 onion
- 2 cloves garlic
- 1 tin red peppers
- 1 bay leaf
- 125 ml (8 tbsp) olive oil
- Salt

Preparation

Soak the chickpeas overnight in lightly salted water.

Place the chickpeas in a pan and cover with fresh water, along with the bay leaf, the beef bone, salt and two tablespoons of olive oil, and cook for around two hours. Meanwhile, chop the onion and garlic and sauté in olive oil until brown, then dice the pork fat and ham, add to the onion and gently fry for a few minutes before adding the peppers cut into strips and removing from the heat.

Once the chickpeas are soft, add them to the pan, removing the bone and the bay leaf. Stir well and cook for a few more minutes, checking for salt before serving.

GARBANZOS CON BACALAO Y ESPINACAS
CHICKPEAS WITH COD AND SPINACH

Ingredients (serves four)

- 500 g (1 lb) chickpeas
- 300 g (10 oz) cod
- 300 g (10 oz) spinach
- 1 onion
- 1 clove garlic
- 3 tomatoes
- 1 bay leaf
- 1 tablespoon paprika
- 150 ml (1/4 pint) olive oil
- Salt

Preparation

Cut the cod into pieces and soak for 24 hours in plenty of cold water, changing the water at least four times.

The chickpeas also need to be soaked overnight, in a separate bowl.

Rinse the chickpeas and place in a pan along with a bay leaf, a little olive oil and salt. Cover with water and cook for around two hours until the chickpeas are tender (add more hot water if needed).

Meanwhile, finely chop the onion and garlic and sauté in olive oil. When they begin to brown, add the peeled chopped tomatoes and leave to cook a few more minutes before adding the paprika.

Wash and chop the spinach and cook in boiling salted water for ten minutes, then drain and put to one side.

Remove any skin and bones from the desalted cod, and add to the sauté, all of which, along with the spinach, is then added to the chickpeas. Leave to cook for another hour, checking for salt. Can be served with a garnish of hardboiled egg.

GUISANTES CON JAMÓN
PEAS WITH HAM

Ingredients (serves four)

- 600 g (1¹/₄ lb) peas
- 200 g (7 oz) ham
- 2 potatoes
- 1 onion
- 3 cloves garlic
- 1 carrot
- 2 eggs
- 3 glasses meat stock
- 100 ml (7 tbsp) olive oil
- Salt

Preparation

Slice the garlic and fry in olive oil, then remove and put to one side.

Use the same oil to gently cook the finely chopped onion and the carrot, also chopped. When they are done add the diced ham and sauté for a minute along with the garlic. Now add the peas, cover with the stock (stock cubes can be used), season and leave to cook gently until the peas are soft.

Meanwhile, peel the potatoes and cut into even pieces, season and fry in olive oil, then remove and add to the cooked peas.

Can be served with a garnish of sliced hardboiled egg.

HABAS SALTEADAS
SAUTÉED BEANS

Ingredients (serves four)

- 1 kg (2 lb) broad beans
- 100 g (3¹/₂ oz) ham
- 100 g (3¹/₂ oz) pork fat
- 2 onions
- 1 lettuce heart
- Ground black pepper
- 75 ml (5 tbsp) olive oil
- Salt

Preparation

Shell the beans and cook them on a low heat in salted water for around thirty minutes, then drain and put to one side.

Meanwhile, chop the onion and sauté in a casserole dish with olive oil. Chop the lettuce in julienne, dice the ham and fat, and add to the onion when it begins to brown.

Add the cooked beans to the frying pan and sauté for a few more minutes, adding black pepper to taste.

JUDÍAS VERDES A LA ESPAÑOLA
SPANISH-STYLE GREEN BEANS

Ingredients (serves four)

- 1 kg (2 lb) green beans
- 100 g (3½ oz) cured ham
- 3 tomatoes
- 500 g (1 lb) potatoes
- 1 onion
- 1 red pepper
- 1 hardboiled egg
- 2 cloves garlic
- 200 ml (⅓ pint) olive oil
- Salt

Preparation

Top and tail the beans, remove any stringy sides and cut into 5 cm (2 inch) pieces. Wash and rinse, then cook in salted boiling water for twenty minutes until soft. Drain and put to one side.

Dice the ham and fry in three tablespoons of olive oil, then remove from the pan and put to one side.

Chop the pepper and onion, slice the garlic, and fry in the same oil, adding the peeled chopped tomatoes when tender.

Meanwhile, peel the potatoes, rinse and dice, then season with salt and fry in plenty of olive oil on a low heat until soft. Remove from the pan, shaking off any excess oil.

Finally, sauté all the ingredients together for three minutes. Turn out into a serving dish, sprinkle with finely chopped hardboiled egg and serve.

LENTEJAS CON CHORIZO
LENTILS WITH CHORIZO SAUSAGE

Ingredients (serves four)

- 300 g (10 oz) lentils
- 1 chorizo sausage
- 150 g (5 oz) pork fat
- 1 onion
- 1 leek

- 2 tomatoes
- 1 green pepper
- 1 carrot
- 2 cloves garlic
- 1 bay leaf

- 1 tsp paprika
- 100 ml (7 tbsp) olive oil
- Salt

Preparation

Place the lentils to soak overnight in water.

The next day, rinse the lentils well, place in a pan and cover with water. Cook on a low heat with a bay leaf and two tablespoons of olive oil. Do not add salt.

Meanwhile, sauté the onion, leek, pepper, finely chopped garlic and sliced carrot in olive oil until brown. Add the peeled and chopped tomatoes and cook for two more minutes, then add the whole mixture to the lentils and cook for around an hour.

Chop the chorizo sausage into slices and the pork fat into strips, and fry gently in a separate pan with olive oil. Remove from the heat and add a teaspoon of paprika, taking care so that it does not burn, then add this mixture to the lentils. Add salt and cook for another five minutes before serving.

MENESTRA
MIXED VEGETABLE STEW

Ingredients (serves four)

- 250 g (9 oz) beef
- 100 g (3 1/2 oz) cured ham
- 250 g (9 oz) broad beans
- 250 g (9 oz) peas
- 200 g (7 oz) green beans

- 6 potatoes
- 6 lettuce leaves
- 4 carrots
- 4 artichokes
- 2 eggs

- 1 onion
- 1 clove garlic
- 4 glasses meat stock
- 1/2 glass white wine
- 200 ml (1/3 pint) olive oil and Salt

Preparation

Chop the onion and garlic and poach in half the olive oil. Chop the beef into pieces, dice the ham and add to the frying pan when the onion is soft. Cook for three minutes and then add the white wine and four glasses of meat stock. Leave to cook until the meat is tender.

Cook the artichokes (remove the outer leaves) on their own in salted water.

Chop the green beans and carrots and add to the meat along with the broad beans, peas and chopped lettuce. Add the artichokes and cook for half an hour until the vegetables are soft.

Meanwhile, peel and dice the potatoes, and fry them in plenty of olive oil. When the stew is ready, add the potatoes, check for salt and cook for five more minutes. The stew can be served with a garnish of hardboiled egg and asparagus.

PASTEL DE PUERROS
LEEK QUICHE

Ingredients (serves four)

- 1 sheet pre-cooked puff pastry
- 6 leeks
- 100 g (3$^{1}/_{2}$ oz) bacon

- 6 eggs
- 10 g ($^{1}/_{2}$ oz) flour
- 125 ml (8 tbsp) olive oil
- Salt

Preparation

Cut the leeks lengthways and rinse with water to remove any dirt caught between the leaves. Dry with a clean cloth and chop into julienne.

Sauté the leeks in olive oil until soft (but not browned), then add the diced bacon and fry for another minute. Season with salt.

Beat the eggs in a bowl and add the leeks and bacon, mixing well.

Dust a tart mould with flour and line with the pastry. Pour the egg mix in and place in the oven preheated to 170° C (340° F) for around twelve minutes until the egg has completely set.

PIMIENTOS ASADOS ALIÑADOS
SEASONED ROAST PEPPERS

Ingredients (serves four)

- 600 g (1 1/4 lb) red peppers
- 3 cloves garlic
- 1 tbsp wine vinegar

- 1 spring onion
- 12 black olives
- 1 tsp chopped parsley

- Ground white pepper
- 200 ml (1/3 pint) olive oil
- Salt

Preparation

Wash and dry the peppers. Roast in a preheated oven at 200° C (390° F) with half of the olive oil. Turn them from time to time, spooning the juice over the top. Remove them from the oven after around twenty minutes, place them in a dish and cover with a cloth until they cool, so they are easier to peel.

Having peeled the peppers, open them up lengthways and remove the stalks and seeds. Use a spoon to remove any remaining seeds.

Slice the peppers and place them in a bowl along with the juices. Now prepare the dressing: finely chop the garlic, slice the spring onion in rings and mix with the vinegar, olives, pepper to taste, salt and the rest of the olive oil. Pour over the peppers, stirring well, sprinkle with chopped parsley and serve.

PIMIENTOS RELLENOS DE ARROZ
PEPPERS STUFFED WITH RICE

Ingredients (serves four)

- 4 peppers (red or green)
- 2 cups rice
- 200 g (7 oz) minced beef
- 1 onion

- 2 cloves garlic
- 1 tomato
- 1 carrot
- 1 glass meat stock

- 100 ml (7 tbsp) olive oil
- Salt

Preparation

Wash the peppers and remove the tops with a circular cut around the stalk. Remove the heart and seeds.

Finely chop half an onion and two cloves of garlic and fry in half of the olive oil. After three minutes add the peeled chopped tomato, leave to cook then add the mince (previously seasoned) and sauté before removing from the heat.

In a saucepan, sauté the rice in a little olive oil before pouring in three cups of water with salt. Cook until the water is absorbed but the rice still slightly hard, as it will finish cooking while the peppers are roasting. Leave to sit for five minutes.

Mix the rice with the meat and use this mixture to stuff the peppers, placing them in an ovenproof dish.

For the sauce, finely chop the remaining half of the onion and the carrot, and fry in three tablespoons of olive oil. When they are soft, add the stock and boil for two minutes.

Pour this sauce over the peppers and place in the oven, preheated to 180° C (360° F) for three quarters of an hour, spooning the sauce over the peppers several times. Serve hot.

PIMIENTOS RELLENOS DE CENTOLLO
PEPPERS STUFFED WITH SPIDER CRAB

Ingredients (serves four)

- 12 sweet red peppers
- 1 spider crab, 1^1/$_2$ kg (3^1/$_2$ lb)
- 1 onion

- 4 tbsp tomato sauce
- ^{1}/$_2$ tbsp flour
- 1 glass fish stock

- ^{1}/$_2$ glass white wine
- 200 ml (^{1}/$_3$ pint) olive oil
- Salt

Preparation

Place the crab in a pan, cover with salted water, bring to the boil and simmer for fifteen minutes, then remove and leave to cool. Extract the meat from the body and the legs and put to one side.

Finely chop half the onion and fry in 50 ml (3 tbsp) of olive oil until crystal clear, then add the crab meat, stir and sauté for a minute before removing from the heat and putting to one side.

Prepare the sauce: Finely chop the other half of the onion in 50 ml (3 tbsp) of olive oil, then add 4 tablespoons of tomato sauce, half a tablespoon of flour, the fish stock and wine. Mix well and cook for fifteen minutes to reduce.

While the sauce is cooking, stuff the peppers with the crab meat, then coat in flour, dip in egg and fry in very hot olive oil. Arrange the peppers on a platter, cover with the piping hot sauce and serve.

POTAJE DE GARBANZOS
CHICKPEA STEW

Ingredients (serves four)

- 500 g (1 lb) chickpeas
- 1 morcilla blood sausage
- 1 chorizo sausage
- 100 g (3¹/₂ oz) pork belly
- 100 g (3¹/₂ oz) green beans

- 2 chard leaves
- 1 onion
- 3 cloves garlic
- 1 potato
- 1 carrot

- 1 green pepper
- 1 tomato
- 1 tbsp paprika
- 100 ml (7 tbsp) olive oil
- Salt

Preparation

Soak the chickpeas overnight in lightly salted water.

Clean and chop the vegetables. The peeled potatoes should be cut into wedges, and the carrots sliced.

Cover the bottom of a pan with olive oil and sauté the chopped onion and pepper. After two minutes add the peeled chopped tomato, the green beans, chard, garlic and carrot. Cook for a few minutes before adding a spoonful of paprika, the chickpeas and the sausage. Cover with water and cook on a low heat for two hours. Add the potatoes twenty minutes before the end, and simmer until both potatoes and chickpeas are soft. Check for salt before serving.

POTE ASTURIANO
ASTURIAN STEW

Ingredients (serves four)

- 200 g (7 oz) white beans or "fabes"
- 100 g (3¹/₂ oz) lacón (pork shoulder)

- 150 g (5 oz) pork fat
- 2 chorizo sausages
- 2 morcilla blood sausages
- 500 g (1 lb) potatoes

- 1 handful cabbage
- 40 ml (3 tbsp) olive oil
- Salt

Preparation

Soak the beans and lacón overnight in water.

Place the beans in a casserole dish together with the sausages, the pork fat and the lacón. Add three tablespoons of olive oil, cover with water and cook for around three hours (the time will depend on the type of beans).

Wash the cabbage and chop in julienne. Cook in boiling water, then rinse and put to one side. Peel and chop the potatoes.

When the beans are almost done, add the potatoes and cook for another twenty minutes, adding more cold water if needed to ensure the ingredients are always covered by liquid. When the potatoes are soft, add the cabbage and stir well, taking care not to split the beans. Check for salt before serving, bearing in mind that the sausages and pork all contain salt.

CHAMPIÑONES A LAS FINAS HIERBAS
MUSHROOMS WITH FINE HERBS

Ingredients (serves four)

- 600 g (1 1/4 lb) mushrooms
- 1/2 tsp rosemary
- 1 tsp thyme
- 1/2 lemon
- 3 cloves garlic
- Ground black pepper
- 200 ml (1/3 pint) olive oil
- Salt

Preparation

Clean the mushrooms with a cloth and remove the sandy stalks. Cut any large mushrooms into pieces, leaving the smaller ones whole.

In a bowl, mix the olive oil, rosemary, thyme, pepper and sliced garlic. Add the mushrooms, coating them evenly, and place in the refrigerator to marinate for three hours.

After this time, fry the mushrooms along with the marinade on a high heat until all the liquid is evaporated. Sprinkle with salt, drizzle a little lemon over and serve.

HUEVOS A LA PROVENZAL
PROVENÇAL EGGS

Ingredients (serves four)

- 4 eggs
- 4 tomatoes
- 2 cloves garlic
- Ground pepper

- 1 tsp chopped parsley
- 150 ml (¼ pint) olive oil
- Salt

Preparation

Wash the tomatoes, dry with a cloth and remove the top of each one.

Chop the garlic, brown in olive oil then remove and put to one side.

In the same pan, with the remaining oil (on a low heat), place the tomatoes, first with the tops facing down, and then facing up, for five minutes on each side. When they are soft, extract the flesh with a teaspoon, leaving a hollow for the eggs.

Place the tomatoes in an ovenproof dish, season with salt and pepper, and break an egg into each one, making sure the yolk remains intact.

Place in the oven preheated to 200° C (390° F) for ten minutes until the eggs set.

Remove from the oven when ready, sprinkle with chopped parsley and serve piping hot.

HUEVOS A LA REINA
QUEEN-STYLE EGGS

Ingredients (serves four)

- 4 eggs
- 100 g (3 1/2 oz) cured ham
- 4 slices bread
- 1 onion

- 6 tbsp tomato sauce
- 1/2 glass cream
- 1/2 glass white wine
- Nutmeg

- White pepper
- 100 ml (7 tbsp) olive oil
- Salt

Preparation

Lightly grease four small cake tins and break an egg into each one, taking care to leave the yolk intact. Season lightly with salt and pepper.

Cover each tin with foil and place in an ovenproof dish or baking tray, then pour boiling water into the dish until it reaches halfway up the cake tins. Place in the oven at 180° C (360° F) for five minutes until the whites are set and the yolks still soft.

Meanwhile, cut the bread slices into circles the same size as the cake tins and fry in olive oil, then remove from the pan and place on kitchen paper to absorb any excess oil.

Use the same pan to brown the onion, finely chopped, then add the diced ham, stir well and pour in the tomato sauce and the white wine. Simmer for five minutes to reduce the liquid, then add the cream and stir well to form a creamy sauce. Add a pinch of nutmeg, check for salt and leave to cook for two more minutes.

Tip the eggs over onto the bread, cover with the sauce and serve piping hot.

HUEVOS CON TORTOS A LA ASTURIANA
ASTURIAS-STYLE EGGS WITH FRITTER CAKES

Ingredients (serves four)

- 4 eggs
- 350 g (11 oz) minced pork
- 150 g (5 oz) minced beef
- 400 g (13 oz) corn flour
- 75 g (3 oz) wheat flour
- 5 cloves garlic
- 2 tsp paprika
- 1/2 tsp chilli pepper
- 300 ml (2/3 pint) olive oil
- Salt

Preparation

Crush the garlic in a mortar and mix with the spices and salt. Add this to the two types of mince, mix well and leave to sit for four or five hours.

Meanwhile, mix the two forms of flour in a bowl. Pour in boiling salted water, bit by bit, stirring with a wooden spoon at first, and then with your hands as it takes on consistency, adding water until the dough does not stick to your hands.

Use this dough to form balls the size of an egg. Place these on a clean, damp cloth and flatten to form thin pancakes.

Fry the cakes on both sides in plenty of very hot oil until brown.

Grease a frying pan with a little olive oil and fry the mince until in pieces and browned.

Fry the eggs in plenty of olive oil, remove and place over the fritter cakes. Serve accompanied with the mince.

HUEVOS REBOZADOS
EGGS IN BATTER

Ingredients (serves four)

- 4 eggs
- 1 egg for the batter
- 4 tbsp flour

- 400 ml (11 fl oz) milk
- 1/2 onion
- 75 g (3 oz) bacon

- 100 g (3 1/2 oz) breadcrumbs
- 200 ml (1/3 pint) olive oil
- Salt

Preparation

Boil the four eggs for twelve minutes, then remove from the pan and cool with cold water. Peel and chop lengthways, then put to one side.

Finely chop the onion and fry in 75 ml (5 tbsp) of olive oil. When it is soft add the diced bacon, sauté for one more minute and put to one side.

Prepare a béchamel sauce by heating four tablespoons of olive oil in a pan and gently frying the flour, then add the milk, a little at a time, stirring constantly with a wooden spoon to prevent lumps. Cook for ten minutes until thick, then season with salt and add the onion and bacon.

Place each egg half in a spoon and dip into the sauce, then remove and allow to cool on the work surface.

Once cold, coat in breadcrumbs, dip in beaten egg and coat again in breadcrumbs, then fry in plenty of olive oil until brown.

REVUELTO DE GAMBAS Y PUERROS
SCRAMBLED EGGS WITH PRAWNS AND LEEK

Ingredients (serves four)

- 300 g (10 oz) prawns
- 4 leeks
- 1 onion
- 2 cloves garlic

- 5 eggs
- 125 ml (8 tbsp) olive oil
- Salt

Preparation

Peel the raw prawns and put to one side.

Slice the garlic, fry in olive oil until brown, then remove and put to one side.

Chop the leek into thin slices and chop the onion. Fry in the same oil, and when they are done (but not brown), add the prawns and cook until they cease to be transparent. Season and add the eggs, without beating, stirring with a wooden spoon until the eggs set.

SETAS A LA CREMA
WILD MUSHROOMS WITH CREAM

Ingredients (serves four)

- 500 g (1 lb) wild (pleurotus eryngii) mushrooms
- 1 onion
- 2 cloves garlic

- 100 g (3¹/₂ oz) bacon
- 250 ml (¹/₂ pint) cream
- Ground black pepper
- 1 chilli pepper (optional)

- 100 ml (7 tbsp) olive oil
- Salt

Preparation

Clean the mushrooms with a cloth and slice thinly. Cut the bacon into strips, and finely chop the garlic and onion.

Gently fry the onion and garlic in half the olive oil, then add the bacon and sauté.

In a separate frying pan, sauté the mushrooms in a little olive oil until all the juice released is reduced.

Now add the onion and bacon to the mushrooms, pour in the cream, season with salt and pepper and cook for five minutes on a moderate heat. Add a chilli pepper for a spicier taste.

TORTA VEGETAL
VEGETABLE OMELETTE

Ingredients (serves four)

- 6 egg
- 200 g (7 oz) carrots
- 1 onion
- 1 courgette

- 1 red pepper
- 2 cloves garlic
- 6 cooked wild asparagus
- 1 tsp chopped parsley

- 50 ml (3 tbsp) olive oil
- Salt

Preparation

Cut the courgette into slices, chop the onion in rings and the pepper in strips, chop the garlic into thin slices and grate the carrot.

Sauté all the vegetables in the olive oil on a low heat until tender but still whole. Add salt.

Beat the eggs in a bowl, adding a little salt.

Sauté the asparagus along with the other vegetables for a few minutes, then pour the egg over the top. Cook on the very lowest heat possible until the egg has set on all sides.

TORTILLA SORPRESA
VEGETABLE OMELETTE

Ingredients (serves four)

- 8 eggs
- 100 g (3^1/$_2$ oz) cured ham, in slices
- 100 g (3^1/$_2$ oz) prawns

- 50 g (2 oz) peas
- 2 tomatoes
- 2 potatoes

- ^{1}/$_4$ tsp oregano
- 100 ml (7 tbsp) olive oil
- Salt

Preparation

Peel the potatoes, cut into thin slices and sprinkle lightly with salt.

Fry on a low heat in the olive oil until soft, then remove from the oil and put to one side.

Cook the peas in boiling salted water for five minutes, then drain and sauté along with the prawns in the same oil used to fry the potatoes.

Meanwhile, cut the tomato into slices. Rub a little olive oil in a frying pan and place the tomato slices in, cooking briefly on both sides, then remove and put to one side.

Beat the eggs, season and pour into a frying pan with a little olive oil. Cook gently until the omelette forms on one side. Over this place the ham, potatoes, peas prawns and finally the slices of tomato. Fold the omelette over, in the manner of a French omelette, to allow the ingredients to set with the egg inside.

ARROZ CASERO
HOME-STYLE RICE

Ingredients (serves four)

- 4 small cups rice
- 200 g (7 oz) lean pork
- 200 g (7 oz) white and red sausages

- 2 tomatoes
- 1 green pepper
- 100 g (3½ oz) cured ham
- 1 tsp paprika

- 3 cloves garlic
- 10 cups meat stock
- 100 ml (7 tbsp) olive oil
- Salt

Preparation

Dice the meat and fry in olive oil, along with the sausages, until brown.

Dice the pepper and add to the pan, along with the ham cut into squares and the garlic in slices. Fry for four minutes and then add the peeled chopped tomato. Add the cups of rice and a spoonful of paprika. Mix well and pour in the boiling fish stock. Check for salt and cook for around seventeen minutes, then leave to sit for five minutes before serving.

ARROZ CON ALMEJAS
CLAMS WITH RICE

Ingredients (serves four)

- 2 cups rice
- 400 g (14 oz) clams
- ½ onion
- 2 cloves garlic
- 1 tsp parsley
- 4½ cups fish stock
- 70 ml (4 tbsp) olive oil
- Salt

Preparation

Finely chop the onion and garlic and gently fry in half of the olive oil, adding the chopped parsley when the onion is soft. Pour in half a cup of fish stock, bring to the boil and add the clams, removing from the heat when the shells open.

Sauté the rice in a separate pan with the rest of oil. Add the rest of the stock, season and bring to the boil, then add the clams with their sauce. Cook on a low heat for around fifteen minutes, remove from the heat and leave to sit for a few minutes before serving.

CANELONES DE BONITO
TUNA CANNELLONI

Ingredients (serves four)

- 16 sheets cannelloni pasta
- 2 tins skipjack tuna in oil
- 1 tin foie-gras
- 1 tin red bell peppers

- 1 onion
- 5 tbsp tomato sauce
- 500 ml (1 pint) milk
- 5 tbsp flour

- $1/2$ tsp oregano
- 50 g (2 oz) grated cheese
- 125 ml (8 tbsp) olive oil
- Salt

Preparation

Finely chop the onion, slice the pepper and drain the tuna. Fry the onion on a low heat with 75 ml (5 tbsp) of olive oil, and when it is tender add the pepper, tuna, foie-gras and tomato sauce. Stir well, add the oregano and put to one side.

Cook the pasta sheets in plenty of boiling salted water for around twelve to fourteen minutes, then drain and lay out on a clean cloth. Place two spoonfuls of filling on each sheet, then wrap these up into tubes and place in an ovenproof dish lightly greased with oil.

Prepare a béchamel sauce. Heat 50 ml (3 tbsp) of olive oil in a pan, then add the flour and stir well for two minutes before gradually adding the milk, stirring constantly to prevent lumps. Cook for a further ten minutes, stirring all the time to prevent the sauce from sticking. Season with salt and pour over the cannelloni, then sprinkle with grated cheese and place under the grill to brown for around ten minutes before serving.

EMPANADA DE BOQUERONES
ANCHOVY PIE

Ingredients (serves four)

For the dough:
- 1 glass olive oil
- 1 glass white wine
- 700 g (1 1/2 lb) flour
- Salt

For the filling:
- 750 g (1 3/4 lb) anchovies
- 1 1/2 onions
- 1 green pepper
- 10 tbsp tomato sauce

- 1 egg
- 75 ml (5 tbsp) olive oil
- Salt

Preparation

Mix the olive oil, white wine and salt in a bowl and beat with a fork until creamy, then gradually add the flour, stirring constantly until the dough can be spread out without sticking to the rolling pin. Leave in a cool place to sit for half an hour.

Clean the anchovies by removing the head, scales and bone, then put the fish to one side.

Finely slice the onion, chop the pepper and sauté in olive oil until tender, then add the tomato sauce followed by the anchovies, stirring well for half a minute.

Take the dough and roll out to a thickness of around half a centimetre (quarter of an inch). Grease an ovenproof dish with oil and cover the bottom with half of the dough, letting it hang over the edges slightly. Place the filling on top and cover with the other half of the dough. Close the edges by pressing the dough together, and adorn with any remaining dough in the form of patterns or shapes.

Brush the surface with beaten egg and place in the oven preheated to 180° C (360° F) for thirty minutes.

ESPAGUETIS CON VERDURAS
SPAGHETTI WITH VEGETABLES

Ingredients (serves four)

- 400 g (13 oz) spaghetti
- 1 aubergine
- 1 courgette
- 1 red pepper

- 1 green pepper
- 1 onion
- 2 tomatoes
- 2 cloves garlic

- 100 g (3$^{1}/_{2}$ oz) grated cheese
- $^{1}/_{2}$ tsp oregano
- 150 ml ($^{1}/_{4}$ pint) olive oil
- Salt

Preparation

Dice the aubergine, courgette and peppers. Chop the onion into rings and the garlic into slices. Peel the tomatoes and chop roughly.

Heat the olive oil in a frying pan and add the peppers. After two or three minutes add the aubergine, courgette, garlic and onion. Three minutes later add the tomatoes, then sauté all the vegetables together for ten minutes. Season with salt and put to one side.

Cook the pasta in plenty of boiling salted water and with a little olive oil for ten minutes, stirring occasionally until al dente.

Drain the spaghetti and add the sauce. Sprinkle with the grated cheese and oregano before serving.

FIDEUÁ
NOODLE PAELLA

Ingredients (serves four)

- 400 g (14 oz) thick, short noodles
- 150 g (5 oz) pork ribs
- 150 g (5 oz) chicken pieces
- 150g (5 oz) squid
- 250 g (9 oz) prawns
- 1 l (2 pints) stock
- 1 tomato
- 1 green pepper
- 4 cloves garlic
- Saffron
- 1 tsp paprika
- 200 ml (1/3 pint) olive oil
- Salt

Preparation

Split the garlic cloves in two and brown in a paella dish with olive oil, then remove and crush in a mortar with a little olive oil and a few threads of saffron.

Use the same oil from the paella dish to fry the ribs and chicken, adding a little salt. Remove the meat when done and put to one side.

Sauté the vegetables in the paella dish with the remaining oil: first add the chopped pepper, followed two minutes later by the peeled chopped tomato, and cook for two more minutes. Chop the squid, peel the prawns and add to the pan. Sauté for a couple of minutes before adding the paprika.

Now add the pork ribs and chicken, along with the garlic, saffron and stock. Bring to the boil and add the pasta. Check for salt and cook for around twelve minutes before serving.

LASAÑA DE BERENJENAS
AUBERGINE LASAGNE

Ingredients (serves four)

- 3 aubergines
- 1 onion
- 3 tomatoes
- 1 green pepper
- 500 g (1 lb) mince

- 75 g (3 oz) pâté
- 250 g (9 oz) sliced cheese
- 750 ml (1^1/$_3$ pint) milk
- 150 g (5 oz) flour
- 50 g (2 oz) grated cheese

- 1 tsp oregano
- Ground black pepper
- 150 ml (10 tbsp) olive oil
- Salt

Preparation

Cut the aubergines into slices, season with salt and pepper and sauté in a little olive oil until soft, then remove and put to one side.

Chop the pepper and onion, and sauté in 100 ml (7 tbsp) of olive oil. Peel and chop the tomatoes and add to the pan when the onion becomes clear.

Cook for two minutes before adding the mince and pâté, season with salt, add the oregano and cook for two more minutes.

Cover the bottom of an ovenproof dish with the aubergine, followed by a layer of meat and another of cheese. Repeat this process at least another two times, and finally cover with a béchamel sauce: toast the flour in 30 ml (2 tablespoons) of olive oil, then slowly add the milk, stirring constantly to prevent lumps forming, and cook for five minutes. Season with salt and pour over the lasagne. Sprinkle with grated cheese and place in the oven for five minutes to grill lightly.

MIGAS
FRIED BREAD CROUTONS

Ingredients (serves four)

- 400 g (14 oz) bread (preferably from a rustic loaf)
- 1 chorizo sausage
- 200 g (7 oz) pork belly
- 6 cloves garlic
- 2 green peppers
- 250 ml (1/2 pint) olive oil
- Salt

Preparation

Break the bread (which should be stale) into very small pieces. Sprinkle with lightly salted water, without soaking it, and wrap it up in a clean tea towel for around three to four hours.

Chop the cloves of garlic in half, slice the pepper into strips and fry in a large frying pan with the olive oil. Slice the chorizo and cut the fat into strips, and add to the pan when the peppers are almost cooked. After a few minutes remove all the ingredients from the pan and put to one side, tipping the oil into a container.

Tip the bread into the same frying pan and slowly add the olive oil, stirring constantly with a wooden spoon until the bread is dry but spongy. Add the sauté of peppers and meat, mix well and serve.

PAELLA DE PESCADO Y MARISCO
FISH AND SEAFOOD PAELLA

Ingredients (serves four)

- 4 small cups rice
- 4 langostino prawns
- 250 g (9 oz) open conger eel
- 2 small crabs
- 12 mussels

- 200 g (7 oz) clams
- 200 g (7 oz) squid
- 100 g (3¹/₂ oz) peas
- ¹/₂ onion
- 1 tomato

- 1 green pepper
- 2 cloves garlic
- Saffron
- 10 cups fish stock
- 150 ml (¹/₄ pint) olive oil and salt

Preparation

Clean the mussels by scraping the shells and rinsing in water. Steam them along with the clams in a pan with a cup of water until the shells open. Strain the resulting stock and put to one side for the rice. Cook the peas on boiling salted water for ten minutes, then put to one side. Cut the conger into pieces, removing any skin and bones. Clean the squid by removing the innards, but keeping the tentacles. Chop into pieces and put to one side.

Chop the pepper, onion and garlic and sauté in olive oil in a paella dish for three minutes, then add the peeled chopped tomatoes. Add the squid and conger eel, and cook for three or four minutes. Now add the rice, stirring well to mix with the other ingredients. Pour in the fish stock and add the ground saffron. Add salt to taste and leave to cook on a high heat for eight minutes. Arrange the prawns, crabs, mussels, clams and peas symmetrically in the pan, and leave to cook for another ten or twelve minutes on a low heat, checking for salt once it has simmered for a while.

Leave to sit for five minutes before serving.

PAELLA DE POLLO
CHICKEN PAELLA

Ingredients (serves four)

- 4 small cups rice
- $^1/_2$ chicken, in pieces
  (as if for frying)
- 1 green pepper
- 1 tin red bell peppers

- 2 tomatoes
- 3 cloves garlic
- 200 g green beans
- $^1/_2$ onion
- $^1/_2$ lemon

- 10 cups chicken stock
- 150 ml ($^1/_4$ pint) olive oil
- Salt

Preparation

Season the chicken pieces and fry in hot oil in a paella dish. When they are brown, add the chopped pepper, onion and garlic. After three minutes, add the peeled chopped tomatoes, mixing well.

Then add the green beans, cooked separately in boiling salted water for ten minutes. Add the rice, mix well with the other ingredients and cook for a couple of minutes.

Now add the boiling stock, bring back to the boil and immediately add the juice of half a lemon. Check for salt and cook on a high heat for ten minutes, and then on a low heat for another seven or eight before removing from the heat.

Leave to sit for five minutes before serving.

TALLARINES MAR Y MONTAÑA
SURF AND TURF PASTA

Ingredients (serves four)

- 400 g (13 oz) noodle pasta
- 12 anchovies in oil
- 500 g (1 lb) mussels
- 50 g (2 oz) black olives

- 150 g (5 oz) mushrooms
- 2 cloves garlic
- 1 tsp chopped parsley
- 1 tsp capers

- 4 tbsp tomato sauce
- $1/2$ tsp oregano
- 125 ml (8 tbsp) olive oil
- Salt

Preparation

Clean the mussels by scraping the shells with a knife and rinsing under the tap. Cook the mussels in a pan with a little water (no salt). Remove from the heat as soon as the open, separating the mussels from their shells once they have cooled a bit, putting the mussels to one side.

Clean the mushrooms with a cloth to remove any sand and cut into slices. Finely chop the garlic and brown in olive oil, then add the mushrooms and sauté for two minutes on a low heat. Chop the olives and add to the pan along with the capers, mussels, anchovies and tomato sauce.

Cook the pasta in plenty of boiling salted water and with a little olive oil for ten minutes, stirring occasionally until al dente. Drain and add the sauce, then sprinkle with chopped parsley and oregano before serving.

ALMEJAS A LA MARINERA
CLAMS WITH GARLIC

Ingredients (serves four)

- 1 kg (2 lb) clams
- 1 large onion
- 4 cloves garlic

- White wine
- Breadcrumbs
- Parsley

- Chilli pepper
- 150 ml ($^1/_4$ pint) olive oil
- Salt

Preparation

Wash the clams several times by scrubbing them in cold water. Discard any dead clams (tap the open shells lightly; the dead clams will not close). Any clams that do not open once cooked should also be discarded.

Finely chop the onion and garlic and fry gently on a low heat in a casserole dish (earthenware if possible) with olive oil until the onion softens. Add a spoonful of fresh parsley crushed in a mortar, a tablespoonful of breadcrumbs, the chilli pepper and a glass and a half of white wine. Season with salt and boil for three minutes. Add the clams and cover the pan until the shells open.

Add water to the sauce if it is too thick, and breadcrumbs if it is too thin.

Serve piping hot in the same casserole dish.

BACALAO A LA RIOJANA
LA RIOJA-STYLE COD

Ingredients (serves four)

- 700 g (1^1/$_2$ lb) cod
- 150 g (5 oz) sweet red pepper
- 3 cloves garlic
- 1 onion
- 2 tomatoes
- 1 tsp chopped parsley
- 100 ml (7 tbsp) olive oil
- Salt

Preparation

Soak the cod in cold water for 24 to 36 hours, depending on the thickness, changing the water three or four times.

Once desalted, place the cod in a casserole dish, cover with cold water and gently heat. Before the water starts to boil, remove from the heat and take out the fish. Remove any skin and bones, and cut into large pieces.

Chop the garlic and onion and fry in olive oil for three minutes, then add the peeled chopped tomato. Cook for ten minutes more before adding the pepper, cut into strips, and half a glass of the strained water used to cook the cod. Simmer for two or three minutes and add salt to taste.

In a casserole dish (preferably earthenware), place a layer of peppers, followed by another of tomatoes and a third of cod, repeating this process and finishing with a layer of peppers and tomatoes.

Place in the oven, preheated to 180° C (360° F) for twenty minutes, then remove and sprinkle with chopped parsley. Serve hot in the same dish.

BACALAO AL PIL PIL
SALT COD PIL PIL

Ingredients (serves four)

- 8 pieces of salt cod, weighing 150 g (5 oz) each
- 1 head of garlic
- 750 ml (1 1/4 pints) olive oil

Preparation

Desalt the cod by soaking in cold water for 24 to 36 hours, depending on the thickness of the pieces, changing the water four times. After this time, drain well and pat dry with a clean cloth.

Finely slice the garlic and brown in a casserole dish (preferably earthenware) with the olive oil, then remove and put to one side.

In the same oil, which should be hot but not bubbling, place the cod with the skin facing down, and shake the pan continuously with a circular motion, until the gelatine is released and the sauce covers most of the cod.

The cooking time will depend on the type of cod used.

Serve in the same dish, with the fried garlic arranged over the top.

BACALAO FRESCO A LA VINAGRETA
FRESH COD À LA VINAIGRETTE

Ingredients (serves four)

- 1 kg (2 lb) fresh cod fillets
- 1 tin sweet red peppers
- 1 spring onion
- 1 green pepper

- 1 egg
- 1 lemon
- 50 g (2 oz) flour
- 300 ml (a little over 1/2 pint) olive oil

- Black pepper
- Salt

Preparation

Chop the spring onion and green pepper in rings. Add the juice of half a lemon, a cup of olive oil and a pinch of salt and pepper. Mix well and put to one side.

Cut the cod into even pieces and season. Coat the pieces in flour, dip in egg and fry in very hot oil until brown.

Arrange the red peppers sliced open on a platter, placing the cod on top. Pour the vinaigrette over the fish and serve.

BERBERECHOS EN SALSA RUBIA
COCKLES IN SAUCE

Ingredients (serves four)

- 1 kg (2 lb) cockles
- 1/4 glass white wine
- 1 tbsp flour
- 1 onion

- 2 cloves garlic
- 1 tsp chopped parsley
- 100 ml (7 tbsp) olive oil
- Salt

Preparation

Place the cockles in cold water for half an hour to draw out any sand. Discard any with their shells open and which do not close when tapped.

Once washed, cook the cockles in a pan with a glass of water. Once the shells open, remove from the pan and put to one side, and strain the cooking water through a muslin.

Finely chop the onion and fry in a casserole dish with olive oil. Crush the garlic in a mortar, mix with the white wine and add to the onion, along with the flour and the cooking water. Season with salt, stir well and cook for five minutes before adding the cockles. Mix with the sauce and cook for two or three more minutes. Serve hot, sprinkled with chopped parsley.

BOQUERONES MARINADOS
MARINATED ANCHOVIES

Ingredients (serves four)

- 700 g (1 1/2 lb) anchovies
- 1 clove garlic
- 1 onion

- 1/2 tsp paprika
- 1 bay leaf
- 50 ml (3 tbsp) sherry vinegar

- 2 tsp chopped parsley
- 250 ml (1/2 pint) olive oil
- Salt

Preparation

Clean the anchovies by removing the heads and extracting the innards. Rinse in cold water and dry well with a clean cloth.

Sprinkle with salt and fry in olive oil for half a minute on each side. Remove and place in a casserole dish.

Use the same oil to sauté a garlic clove (left whole) and an onion chopped into rings; when they begin to clear remove from the heat and add the paprika, bay leaf and vinegar.

Add this mixture to the anchovies and leave to marinate for twenty-four hours.

The next day, check for salt and sprinkle with chopped parsley.

Serve cold.

CABALLA AL HORNO
ROAST MACKEREL

Ingredients (serves four)

- 2 large mackerel
- 1 lemon
- 10 ml (1 tbsp) vinegar
- 2 cloves garlic
- 100 ml (7 tbsp) olive oil
- Salt

Preparation

Clean the fish and remove the heads. Open the fish up like a book by making a cut along the belly, with the spine remaining attached to one of the sides.

Grease an ovenproof dish with olive oil and place the fish in, drizzle with the juice of the lemon and season with salt. Place in the oven, preheated to 180° C (360° F) for ten minutes.

While the mackerel is roasting, slice the garlic and brown in olive oil, then remove from the heat and add the vinegar.

Remove the fish from the oven, pour the oil and garlic over the top and serve immediately.

CALAMARES EN SALSA
SQUID IN SAUCE

Ingredients (serves four)

- 1 kg (2 lb) squid
- 1 onion
- 3 hardboiled eggs
- 4 cloves garlic

- 100 g (3^1/$_2$ oz) pork fat
- 4 tomatoes
- 1 tsp chopped parsley
- 100 g (3^1/$_2$ oz) pitted olives

- 1 glass white wine
- 150 ml (^{1}/$_4$ pint) olive oil
- Salt

Preparation

Clean the squid, discarding the head and innards. Rinse the body sac with water and leave whole. Cut the tentacles into small pieces.

Chop half the onion and fry in 3 tablespoons of olive oil, then add the squid tentacles and the finely chopped pork fat, and cook for three minutes. Remove from the heat and add the chopped hardboiled eggs and the diced olives. Use this mixture to stuff the squid bodies, closing them with a toothpick.

Finely chop the garlic, the other onion half and the peeled tomatoes and sauté in a casserole dish with 7 tablespoons of olive oil. Place the squid over the sauté, pour in the wine, season and cook for twenty minutes. Add a little water if the sauce becomes too thick.

Sprinkle with chopped parsley and serve.

CALAMARES EN SU TINTA
SQUID IN INK

Ingredients (serves four)

- 1¹/₂ kg (3¹/₂ lb) squid
- 2 cloves garlic
- 1 onion
- 3 tbsp tomato sauce
- ¹/₂ tsp chopped parsley
- ¹/₂ glass white wine
- 3 sachets squid ink
- ¹/₂ cup milk
- 100 ml (7 tbsp) olive oil
- Salt

Preparation

Clean the squid, discarding the heads but keeping the tentacles, and cut into slices and pieces.

Finely chop the onion, garlic and parsley and sauté in olive oil.

When the onion is soft, add the squid and mix in. Now add the tomato and white wine, and cook on a low heat for thirty minutes.

Meanwhile, dilute the squid ink in the milk and add to the pan when the squid is tender. Mix well and cook for five more minutes.

Check for salt, bearing in mind that the squid ink is quite salty.

Can be served with boiled rice.

CONGRIO CON PATATAS Y GUISANTES
CONGER EEL WITH POTATOES AND PEAS

Ingredients (serves four)

- 4 slices conger eel from the open part of the fish, weighing 300 g (10 oz) each
- 750 g (1 3/4 lb) potatoes
- 400 g (14 oz) peas
- 2 cloves garlic
- 2 tsp chopped parsley
- 1 onion
- 1/2 glass white wine
- 50 g (2 oz) flour
- 250 ml (1/2 pint) olive oil
- Salt

Preparation

Season the fish, coat in flour and fry in 3 tablespoons of hot olive oil, then remove and place in an earthenware casserole dish.

Peel the potatoes and cut into thick slices, season and fry in 200 ml (1/3 pint) of olive oil, gently at first until soft, and then on a higher heat.

Arrange the potatoes around the fish in the casserole dish.

Finely chop the onion and garlic and fry in the same pan used to fry the fish, with the rest of the olive oil. Chop the parsley and add to the onion when it is soft, along with the white wine. Cook the peas in boiling salted water for seven minutes, then add to the pan.

Cover the fish with this sauce and cook on a low heat for five minutes before serving.

CONGRIO EN SALSA VERDE
CONGER EEL IN GREEN SAUCE

Ingredients (serves four)

- 4 slices conger eel, opened, around 300 g (10 oz) each
- 1 tbsp chopped parsley
- 3 cloves garlic
- $1/2$ tbsp flour
- $1/2$ glass white wine
- 100 ml (7 tbsp) olive oil
- Salt

Preparation

Finely chop the garlic and fry in olive oil in a casserole dish, preferably earthenware. When the garlic begins to brown, add the parsley and the flour, stirring constantly with a wooden spoon, adding the white wine once the flour has been evenly absorbed.

Boil for a minute before adding the seasoned fish, and cook for around a quarter of an hour. Add more water if the sauce becomes too thick.

DORADA A LA ESPALDA
GRILLED SPLIT GILT-HEAD

Ingredients (serves four)

- 4 portion-sized gilt-head
- 2 lemons
- 6 cloves garlic

- 2 tsp chopped parsley
- 200 ml (¹/₃ pint) olive oil
- Salt

Preparation

Clean and scale the fish, then open them up by cutting from the belly towards the tail. Place them opened up on a baking tray, drizzle with the juice of the lemons and season. Cut the garlic into slices and place over the fish.

Heat the oil in a frying pan and when it begins to smoke, pour over the fish. Sprinkle with chopped parsley and place in the oven, preheated to 180° C (360° F) for fifteen minutes, pouring the sauce over the fish several times during the cooking.

LENGUADO EN CACHOPO RELLENO
SOLE CORDON BLEU

Ingredients (serves four)

- 1 kg (2 lb) sole fillets
- 100 g (3¹/₂ oz) cured ham, in slices
- 200 g (7 oz) prawns
- 200 g (7 oz) clams
- 1 onion
- 1 egg
- 2 cloves garlic
- 50 g (2 oz) flour
- 1 glass white wine
- 1 tsp chopped parsley
- 150 ml (¹/₄ pint) olive oil
- Salt

Preparation

Make a cut down the middle of the fillets, without cutting them entirely, in order to fold them like a book. Season lightly with salt.

Peel three raw prawns per fillet and put to one side.

Place a slice of ham over one half of each fillet of sole, trimming the edges, and then the three prawns. Close the fillets over with the other half, coat in flour and then dip in egg.

Fry the fillets in olive oil on both sides until brown. Remove from the pan and place in a casserole dish.

Filter the oil and fry the finely chopped onion. When it begins to clear, add the garlic and parsley, crushed in a mortar and mixed with a glass of white wine. Boil for a couple of minutes then pour over the fish. Arrange the clams and the remaining prawns around the fillets and cook for five more minutes before serving.

LUBINA CON SALSA DE ORICIOS
SEA BASS WITH SEA URCHIN SAUCE

Ingredients (serves four)

- 4 sea bass steaks, 250 g (9 oz) each
- 2 leeks
- 1 tin sea urchin caviar
- 1 onion
- 2 carrots
- 3 cloves garlic
- 1 glass white wine
- 1 cup fish stock
- 4 langostino prawns
- 100 ml (7 tbsp) olive oil
- Salt

Preparation

Chop the onion, carrots and the white part of the leeks and sauté in olive oil. When they are soft, liquefy with a blender and add the white wine and fish stock. Bring to the boil and simmer for a minute before adding the caviar and seasoning with salt.

Season the fish and place on a baking tray, then pour the sauce over. Arrange the prawns on the top and place in the oven, preheated to 180° C (360° F) for twelve minutes.

LUBINA CON VERDURAS
SEA BASS WITH VEGETABLES

Ingredients (serves four)

- 1 $^1/_4$ kg (2 $^3/_4$ lb) sea bass fillets
- 250 g prawns
- 8 clams
- 1 onion

- 1 red pepper
- 1 leek
- 2 tomatoes
- $^1/_2$ glass brandy

- $^1/_2$ l (1 $^1/_4$ pints) fish stock
- 150 ml (10 tbsp) olive oil
- Salt

Preparation

Chop all the vegetables in julienne.

Sauté the pepper, leek and onion in the olive oil for two minutes, then add the peeled chopped tomatoes and cook for two minutes more.

Pour in the brandy and fish stock, bring to boil, simmer for five minutes and season.

Season the fish and place in an ovenproof dish along with the prawns and clams, pouring the vegetable sauce over the top.

Place in the oven, preheated to 180° C (360° F) for around eight minutes.

MARMITA DE SALMÓN
SALMON CASSEROLE

Ingredients (serves four)

- 1 kg (2 lb) potatoes
- 500 g (1 lb) salmon
- 1 onion
- 1 green pepper
- 1 red pepper
- 2 tomatoes
- 1/2 glass brandy
- 3 glasses fish stock
- 100 ml (7 tbsp) olive oil
- Salt

Preparation

Chop the onion and pepper and sauté in a casserole dish with olive oil. After a few minutes add the peeled chopped tomatoes, and cook gently without the ingredients browning.

Peel and dice the potatoes and add them to the casserole dish. Cook for three minutes before adding the brandy and covering the potatoes with the fish stock, which can be made using the bones and skin from the salmon.

Cut the salmon into even pieces and add to the dish, along with salt, once the potatoes are soft (around twenty minutes). Cover the dish and cook for two or three minutes, which should be long enough for the salmon to be cooked through.

MEJILLONES EN SALSA PICANTE
MUSSELS IN SPICY SAUCE

Ingredients (serves four)

- 2 kg (4$^1/_2$ lb) mussels
- 6 cloves garlic
- 2 leeks

- 1 chilli pepper
- 2 tomatoes
- $^1/_2$ tsp paprika

- Ground black pepper
- 100 ml (7 tbsp) olive oil
- Salt

Preparation

Chop the garlic and brown in the olive oil for a minute, then add the chopped leeks and tomatoes, along with the chilli pepper. Season and cook on a low heat for ten minutes.

Meanwhile, clean the mussels by scraping the shells with a knife. Rinse in cold water, discarding any which are broken and which if open do not close when tapped.

Tip the mussels into a pan and cook with a glass of unsalted water until the shells open. Leave each mussel in one half of its shell, removing and discarding the other half. Place the mussels in a serving dish and put the cooking water to one side.

Add the paprika and half a glass of the cooking water to the vegetables. Mix well and cover the mussels with this sauce. Sprinkle with black pepper and serve.

MEJILLONES EN SALSA VERDE
MUSSELS IN GREEN SAUCE

Ingredients (serves four)

- 2^1/$_2$ kg (5^1/$_2$ lb) mussels
- 1^1/$_2$ onions
- 3 cloves garlic
- 1 tbsp chopped parsley

- 1 glass white wine
- 150 ml (^{1}/$_4$ pint) olive oil
- 1 chilli pepper (optional)
- Salt

Preparation

Clean the mussels by scraping the shells with a knife. Rinse in water and steam in a saucepan with two glasses of water, without salt. When all the mussels have opened, remove from the heat and leave to cool, then extract the mussels and discard the shells.

Finely chop the onion and sauté in a casserole dish (preferably earthenware). Crush the garlic in a mortar, along with the parsley and a glass of white wine. Add this to the onion, simmer for three or four minutes and season to taste.

Finally, add the mussels and cook for five more minutes. Add a little chilli pepper for a spicier taste. Serve hot.

MERLUZA A LA ASTURIANA
ASTURIAS-STYLE HAKE

Ingredients (serves four)

- 4 slices hake, 300 g (10 0z) each one
- 4 cloves garlic
- 1/2 onion

- Tomato sauce
- 50 g (2 oz) flour
- 400 ml (3/4 pint) natural cider
- 1 tsp chopped parsley

- 12 clams
- 12 prawns
- 100 ml (7 tbsp) olive oil
- Salt

Preparation

In a casserole dish (preferably earthenware), sauté the chopped garlic in hot olive oil. When they begin to brown, add the finely chopped onion.

When the onion is ready, add the hake, previously seasoned and coated in flour, and fry gently on both sides.

Add a cup of tomato sauce, the clams and prawns, and cover with the cider. Shake the casserole dish to mix all the ingredients and leave to cook for ten minutes on a medium heat (add a chilli pepper for a spicier flavour).

Sprinkle with parsley and serve.

MERLUZA A LA CAZUELA
HAKE CASSEROLE

Ingredients (serves four)

- 4 slices of hake, 250 g (9 oz) each
- 250 g (9 oz) clams
- 4 asparagus
- 50 g (2 oz) cured ham

- ½ onion
- 100 g (3½ oz) peas
- 3 cloves garlic
- 1 tsp flour
- ½ tsp chopped parsley

- 1 glass fish stock
- 1 glass white wine
- 100 ml (7 tbsp) olive oil
- Salt

Preparation

Season the hake and place in an earthenware casserole dish, with the clams arranged around the fish.

Finely chop the onion and fry in the olive oil. Dice the ham and add to the pan when the onion becomes clear, and gently sauté for a couple of minutes.

Crush the garlic and parsley in a mortar, add the wine and flour and pour this mixture over the onion and ham. Simmer for two minutes before adding the fish stock.

Pour this sauce over the fish, then cook for fifteen minutes, spooning the sauce over the fish several times. Cook the peas in boiling salted water for fifteen minutes, then drain and add to the fish. Place an asparagus over each piece of hake and serve.

MERLUZA CON ANGULAS
HAKE WITH ELVERS

Ingredients (serves four)

- 4 backs of hake, 250 g (9 oz) each
- 200 g elvers (baby eels)

- 4 cloves garlic
- 2 tsp chopped parsley
- 50 g (2 oz) flour

- 1 chilli pepper (optional)
- 200 ml (1/3 pint) olive oil
- Salt

Preparation

Sprinkle the hake pieces with salt and coat in flour.

Lightly brown the hake on both sides in 150 ml (1/4 pint) of olive oil, then place in a lightly greased ovenproof dish and place in the oven preheated to 170° C (340° F) for ten minutes.

Meanwhile, thinly slice the garlic and brown in the rest of the olive oil, and then add the chilli pepper and the elvers. Cook for two minutes before sprinkling with chopped parsley.

Remove the fish from the oven, cover with the elvers and garlic and serve immediately.

MERLUZA CON SALSA MARISCADA
HAKE WITH SEAFOOD SAUCE

Ingredients (serves four)

- 4 hake loins, 300 g (10 oz) each
- 8 langostino prawns
- 1 red pepper
- 1 onion

- 2 tomatoes
- 1/2 tsp parsley
- 50 g (2 oz) flour
- 1 glass brandy

- 1 glass fish stock
- 250 ml (1/2 pint) olive oil
- Salt

Preparation

First prepare the sauce: chop the pepper and onion and fry in 200 ml (1/3 pint) olive oil for five minutes, add the peeled chopped tomatoes and cook for a couple of minutes more.

Peel the prawns and put to one side.

Crush the prawn heads and shells in a mortar with a little fish stock. Sieve this mixture and add to the pan. Pour in the brandy and flambé.

To this sauce, add the rest of the fish stock and four of the prawns. Season and cook for ten minutes, then blend with a mixer and (for a smoother sauce) strain through a colander.

Coat the fish in flour, season and brown in 50 ml (3 tbsp) of olive oil, preferably in an earthenware casserole dish. Place the other four prawns around the fish, pour the sauce over the top and place in an oven preheated to 180° C (360° F) for ten minutes. Sprinkle with chopped parsley before serving.

NAVAJAS AL LIMÓN
RAZOR CLAMS WITH LEMON

Ingredients (serves four)

- 24 razor shell clams
- 1 lemon
- 3 cloves garlic

- 1 tsp parsley
- 100 ml (7 tbsp) olive oil
- Salt

Preparation

Place the razor clams in cold water for half an hour to draw out any sand, then rinse thoroughly under the tap and dry with a clean cloth.

Sauté the clams in olive oil with the finely chopped garlic, then drizzle with lemon juice and leave on a low heat until the liquid is reduced by half.

Season lightly with salt, sprinkle with chopped parsley and serve immediately.

PEZ DE ESPADA CON VERDURAS
SWORDFISH WITH VEGETABLES

Ingredients (serves four)

- 1 kg (2 lb) swordfish
- 1 small aubergine
- 1 onion
- 1 red pepper

- 1 green pepper
- 1 small courgette
- 4 young garlic sprouts
- $1/2$ tsp chopped parsley

- Ground white pepper
- 100 ml (7 tbsp) olive oil
- Salt

Preparation

Chop the aubergine and courgette into large pieces, the onion and garlic in rings and the pepper into squares and sauté the vegetables in olive oil: first the onion and garlic, and then the peppers, aubergine and courgette when the onion begins to clear. Cook for around seven to eight minutes.

Meanwhile, cut the swordfish into squares and season with salt and pepper.

When the vegetables are tender, but still more or less intact, add the fish and sauté for another four or five minutes until done.

Sprinkle with the chopped parsley and serve.

PEZ DE ESPADA EN SALSA DE ALMENDRAS
SWORDFISH IN ALMOND SAUCE

Ingredients (serves four)

- 1¼ kg (2¾ lb) swordfish fillets
- 150 g (5 oz) raw almonds
- 4 cloves garlic

- 1 onion
- 2 tsp chopped parsley
- Ground white pepper

- 1½ glasses white wine
- 150 ml (10 tbsp) olive oil
- Salt

Preparation

Finely chop the onion and garlic, and brown in the olive oil, then add the parsley and the almonds, previously crushed in a mortar.

Season the fish to taste and add to the pan. Sauté lightly on both sides, then pour in the white wine and leave to reduce on a low heat for ten minutes before serving.

PUERRUSALDA DE BACALAO
COD WITH LEEKS AND POTATOES

Ingredients (serves four)

- 200 g (7 oz) cod
- 6 leeks
- 5 potatoes
- 100 ml (7 tbsp) olive oil
- Salt

Preparation

Soak the cod in cold water for 24 hours, changing the water every eight hours. Once desalted, rinse the fish and place in a pan covered with water. Bring to the boil and then remove from the heat and put to one side.

Clean the leeks, discarding the greenest part, and chop into even slices; sauté with the olive oil, and before they take on colour add the peeled and diced potatoes.

Rinse the cod and put to one side. Pour the liquid over the leeks and potatoes, adding more water if necessary to cover the vegetables. Cook until the potatoes are soft.

Remove skin and bones from the cod, flake the flesh into pieces and add to the pan. Boil for a minute, check for salt and serve.

PULPO AL AJILLO
OCTOPUS WITH GARLIC

Ingredients (serves four)

- 1 kg (2 lb) octopus
- 6 cloves garlic
- 1 bay leaf
- 1 chilli pepper
- 150 ml (¼ pint) olive oil
- Salt

Preparation

Thoroughly wash the octopus, rubbing it with cold water to remove any sand in the suckers. Remove the eyes and mouth.

Once clean, place in a pan of boiling water with a bay leaf, then remove and plunge into the water once again, two or three times until the tentacles shrink. Leave to cook for around forty minutes, adding salt a little before the end. The octopus is ready when it can be skewered easily.

Remove from the water and leave to cool, then cut into slices.

Slice the garlic and brown in a casserole dish with olive oil, then add the octopus and chilli pepper. Sauté for three or four minutes, then serve hot in the same dish.

RAGOUT DE CHIPIRONES
RAGOUT OF CUTTLEFISH

Ingredients (serves four)

- 1 kg (2 lb) small cuttlefish
- 700 g (1 1/2 lb) potatoes
- 250 g (9 oz) peas
- 2 onions

- 3 carrots
- 3 cloves garlic
- 1 tsp chopped parsley
- Ground white pepper

- 1 glass white wine
- 150 ml (10 tbsp)olive oil
- Salt

Preparation

Clean the cuttlefish by separating the head from the sac. Remove the innards and the feather from inside the sac and separate the tentacles from the head. Rinse with cold water and drain well. Cut the sacs into three and leave the tentacles intact. Discard all the rest.

Fry the cuttlefish in olive oil, then remove from the pan and put to one side.

Chop the garlic, onion and carrot in the same oil, then add the white wine. Bring to the boil and simmer briefly, then add the cuttlefish. Stir these in, followed by the peas. Cover with water, season to taste and cook on a low heat for twenty minutes.

Meanwhile, peel and dice the potatoes, then fry in olive oil for fifteen minutes. Add to the cuttlefish and mix well. Sprinkle with parsley and leave to sit for three minutes before serving.

RAPE MARINERO
MONKFISH IN A GARLIC AND PARSLEY SAUCE

Ingredients (serves four)

- 1 kg (2 lb) monkfish
- 8 langostino prawns
- 8 clams
- 1 tbsp flour
- 2 cloves garlic
- 1/2 tsp parsley
- 1/2 glass white wine
- 1/2 glass fish stock
- 50 ml (3 tbsp) olive oil
- Salt

Preparation

Cut the fish into thin slices and season with salt.

Slice the garlic and brown in the olive oil in an earthenware casserole dish. In the same dish, sauté the fish and pour in the wine and stock, adding a spoonful of flour to thicken the sauce. Add more salt if needed.

Place the prawns and clams around the fish and sprinkle with chopped parsley, then place in the oven, preheated to 170° C (340° F) for five minutes.

RAYA AL AJO ARRIERO
SKATE WITH GARLIC

Ingredients (serves four)

- 1 kg (2 lb) skate in pieces (skin removed)
- 5 cloves garlic

- 1 tsp paprika
- 4 tsp vinegar
- 2 hardboiled eggs

- 4 potatoes
- 50 ml (3 tbsp) olive oil
- Salt

Preparation

Slice the garlic and fry in olive oil in an earthenware casserole dish. Season the fish and add to the garlic when it begins to brown. Fry on both sides and then add the paprika. Cook on a low heat for around a minute, then pour in the vinegar and remove from the heat.

Can be served with steamed potatoes and chopped hardboiled egg.

REY AL HORNO
ROAST KINGFISH

Ingredients (serves four)

- 1 kingfish/croaker weighing 1 1/2 kg (3 1/2 lb)
- 750 g (1 3/4 lb) potatoes
- 1 onion

- 3 cloves garlic
- 1 glass dry white wine
- 1 lemon
- Ground white pepper

- 1 tsp chopped parsley
- 30 g (1 oz) breadcrumbs
- 200 ml (1/3 pint) olive oil
- Salt

Preparation

Clean the fish, rub with salt, pepper and the juice of the lemon and leave to sit for half an hour.

Meanwhile, peel the potatoes and cut into slice, and finely chop the onions. Season the potatoes and gently fry in olive oil, then add the onion when the potato softens. Turn the heat up and fry until the onion becomes clear, then remove both from the pan and drain of any oil.

Arrange the potato and onion on a baking tray and place the fish over the top.

Cut the garlic into slices and brown them in the same oil used for the potatoes, then pour the oil and garlic over the fish. Sprinkle with the breadcrumbs and parsley and place in the oven, preheated to 180° C (360° F) for twenty minutes, basting the fish with the juices every five minutes.

SALMÓN A LA RIBEREÑA
LA RIBERA-STYLE SALMON

Ingredients (serves four)

- 4 slices salmon, weighing 250 g (9 oz) each
- 100 g (3¹/2 oz) prawns
- 4 ham slices
- 1 glass natural cider
- 1 glass fish stock
- 50 g (2 oz) flour
- 1 onion
- 1 tomato
- 1 carrot
- 100 ml (7 tbsp) olive oil
- Salt

Preparation

Season the salmon with salt and lightly coat in flour. Seal on both sides in a little olive oil, without them browning too much.

Place the salmon in a casserole dish and pour over the cider and fish stock (this can be prepared using the shells of the prawns). Cook on a low heat for three or four minutes.

Meanwhile, prepare the sauce: chop the onion and carrot and sauté in olive oil, adding the peeled chopped tomatoes after three minutes.

Sauté the peeled prawns for half a minute, then blend in a mixer, season and pour this sauce over the salmon. Simmer for another four minutes, shaking the dish to mix the sauce well.

Slice the ham, place over the salmon and serve.

SALMÓN A LA SARTÉN
PAN-FRIED SALMON

Ingredients (serves four)

- 4 salmon slices, weighing 250 g (9 oz) each
- 4 potatoes

- ¹/₂ glass brandy
- ¹/₂ glass white wine
- 2 cloves garlic

- 1 tsp chopped parsley
- 75 ml (5 tbsp) olive oil
- Salt

Preparation

Place the salmon in a shallow dish. Pour the brandy and wine over, and leave to marinate for twenty to thirty minutes, then remove the fish and rub in salt and crushed garlic.

Fry the fish in hot olive oil (but on a low heat) for three minutes on each side. Now add a spoonful of the liqueur used to marinate the fish, one for each slice, and cook for three to four minutes, spooning the juice over the fish from time to time.

Serve sprinkled with chopped parsley and with a side dish of steamed potatoes.

SALMONETES AL JEREZ
RED MULLET IN SHERRY

Ingredients (serves four)

- 4 red mullet fish (1 kg/2 lb in total)
- 1/2 lemon
- 3 cloves garlic

- 1/2 glass sherry
- Ground white pepper
- 50 g (2 oz) breadcrumbs
- 500 g (1 lb) potatoes

- 100 ml (7 tbsp) olive oil
- Salt

Preparation

Clean the fish, removing scales and innards. Rinse with water and pat dry with a clean cloth.

Once, clean, place in an ovenproof dish, brush with olive oil, season with salt and pepper and sprinkle with breadcrumbs. Place in the oven preheated to 180° C (360° F) for fifteen minutes.

Meanwhile, slice the garlic and fry with the rest of the olive oil, then add the juice of half a lemon and half a glass of sherry. Simmer for a couple of minutes then pour over the fish, now out of the oven.

Serve with steamed potatoes.

SALPICÓN DE BUEY DE MAR Y MERLUZA
CRAB AND HAKE SALAD

Ingredients (serves four)

- 1 ox crab weighing 1 1/2 kg (3 1/2 lb)
- 200 g hake
- 1/2 onion
- 1 hardboiled egg
- 1 spring onion
- 1 tin bell red peppers
- 2 tsp chopped parsley
- 50 ml (3 tbsp) sherry vinegar
- 150 ml (1/4 pint) olive oil
- Salt

Preparation

With the crab still alive, place it in a pan and cover it with cold water and a good handful of salt. Bring to the boil and simmer for around twelve minutes, then remove and leave to cool.

Meanwhile, cook the hake in a pan with water, salt, a piece of onion and a sprig of parsley. Bring to the boil and simmer for to minutes, then remove the fish and put the cooking water to one side. Remove the skin and bones, and crumble the flesh into flakes.

Remove the crab's legs and claws. Use a knife to open up the shell, then cut up the meat from the body legs and claws using a lobster cracker. Extract all the flesh, taking care not to include any bits of shell.

Mix the crab and hake meat, and use this to fill the crab shell.

Prepare a vinaigrette dressing. Chop the hardboiled egg, pepper spring onion and parsley. Add the vinegar, olive oil and a pinch of salt. Mix well and stir into the fish and crab meat.

SARDINAS GUISADAS
STEWED SARDINES

Ingredients (serves four)

- 1 kg (2 lb) sardines
- 1 onion
- 1 green pepper

- 3 tomatoes
- 1/2 tsp paprika
- 1 tsp chopped parsley

- 1/2 glass white wine
- 100 ml (7 tbsp) olive oil
- Salt

Preparation

Chop the onion, cut the pepper into squares and fry for two minutes in the olive oil, then add the peeled chopped tomatoes and cook on a low heat for five or six more minutes.

Meanwhile, clean the sardines by removing the heads and innards, then rinse in cold water and dry with a clean cloth.

Place the sardines in an ovenproof dish greased with a little olive oil, season with salt and put to one side.

Add half a teaspoon of paprika to the paprika and season with salt. Pour over the sardines, along with the wine, and sprinkle with chopped parsley.

Place in the oven, preheated to 180° C (360° F) for five minutes, remove and serve.

SARDINILLAS A LA GABARDINA
SARDINES IN BATTER

Ingredients (serves four)

- 1 kg (2 lb) small sardines
- 300 g (10 oz) flour
- 1 glass beer
- 1 tsp chopped parsley

- 2 egg whites
- 200 ml ($1/3$ pint) olive oil
- Salt

Preparation

Mix the flour, two tablespoons of olive oil, the parsley and salt in a bowl. Slowly pour in the beer and mix to form a smooth, fairly thick paste. Beat the egg whites until stiff, fold into the paste and mix well.

Clean the sardines by removing the heads and guts. Open the fish up and remove the bones. Season and coat with the batter.

Fry in very hot olive oil until brown, remove and serve.

TRUCHA ASALMONADA CON CHAMPIÑONES
ROAST SALMON TROUT WITH MUSHROOMS

Ingredients (serves four)

- 2 salmon trout, 600 g (1 1/4 lb) each
- 300 g (10 oz) mushrooms
- 1 onion

- 1/2 lemon
- 1/2 tsp oregano
- Ground white pepper
- 1 tbsp breadcrumbs

- 1/2 glass natural cider
- 75 ml (5 tbsp) olive oil
- Salt

Preparation

Clean the fish, removing the innards. Rinse well and dry with a clean cloth.

Clean the mushrooms and slice finely, then drizzle with the juice of half a lemon and put to one side.

Finely chop the onion and fry in olive oil until it starts to become transparent, then add the mushrooms and cook on a low heat for ten minutes until soft.

Cover the bottom of an ovenproof dish with the onions and mushrooms, and place the trout over the top. Season with salt, pepper to taste and the oregano, and place in the oven, preheated to 180° C (360° F) for twenty minutes.

After five minutes, drizzle with the cider and sprinkle with the breadcrumbs.

TRUCHAS A LA CAZUELA
TROUT CASSEROLE

Ingredients (serves four)

- 4 ration-sized trout
- 4 slices ham
- 4 cloves garlic
- 4 potatoes
- 1½ onions

- 1 bay leaf
- 1 tsp parsley
- 1 glass white wine
- 150 ml (10 tbsp) olive oil
- Salt

Preparation

Clean the fish, removing the innards and rinsing in water. Pat dry with a clean cloth and sprinkle with salt.

Slice the garlic and brown in olive oil, then remove and place in a casserole dish.

Peel and slice the potatoes, sprinkle with salt and fry in the oil used for the garlic. After four minutes add the chopped onion and continue cooking for five or six more minutes until the onion is soft. Then remove from the pan and tip into the casserole dish, covering the base.

Stuff the fish with the ham and fry for a couple of minutes in the rest of the oil. Place the trout in the casserole dish, pour over the white wine and sprinkle with chopped parsley. Cook for five minutes before serving.

ALBÓNDIGAS DE TERNERA CON QUESO
BEEF MEATBALLS WITH CHEESE

Ingredients (serves four)

- 500 g (1 lb) minced beef
- 100 g (3$\frac{1}{2}$ oz) minced pork
- 1 red pepper
- 1$\frac{1}{2}$ onions
- 2 cloves garlic

- 30 g (1 oz) breadcrumbs
- 1 egg
- 1 sprig parsley
- $\frac{1}{2}$ glass milk
- 75 g (3 oz) flour

- 1 carrot
- 1 glass white wine
- 150 g (5 oz) hard cream cheese
- 200 ml ($\frac{1}{3}$ pint) olive oil
- Salt

Preparation

Gently fry half the pepper, half an onion and a clove of garlic in a quarter of the olive oil, making sure they do not brown. Add the chopped parsley and remove from the heat.

In a bowl, mix the sautéed vegetables with the breadcrumbs (previously soaked in milk), the beaten egg and the seasoned mincemeat.

Dice the cheese into 1 cm ($\frac{1}{2}$ inch) squares.

Use your hands to form the meatballs, sticking a piece of cheese inside each one. Roll them in flour and fry in olive oil until brown, then remove and place in a pan.

Pour half of the oil from frying the meatballs into a new frying pan. Finely chop an onion, half the pepper, a clove of garlic and a carrot and gently fry in the oil, then add the white wine. Cook on a low heat for two minutes, then blend the sauce and pour over the meatballs. Cook the balls and sauce together for twenty-five minutes and serve.

ALETA DE TERNERA RELLENA
STUFFED BRISKET OF BEEF

Ingredients (serves four)

- 750 g (1 3/4 lb) brisket of beef, opened up
- 1 onion
- 1 small tin red bell peppers

- 2 cloves garlic
- 1/4 tsp oregano
- 4 eggs
- 200 g (7 oz) rashers bacon

- 1 glass white wine
- 1 glass brandy
- 250 ml (1/2 pint) olive oil
- Salt

Preparation

Remove and discard any fat from the meat, flatten with a mallet and sprinkle with salt.

Beat the eggs, heat a spoonful of oil in a frying pan and make an omelette, seasoned with oregano.

Spread the meat out and place the omelette over the top. Next place the rashers of bacon and the peppers, cut into strips. Roll the meat up and tie with kitchen twine, taking care so no stuffing is squeezed out.

Brown the roll of meat on all sides in hot oil. Use the same oil to sauté the chopped onion. Crush the garlic in a mortar with the brandy and wine, and add this to the meat when the onion begins to brown. Leave to cook for an hour and a half, adding a little water or white wine if the sauce becomes too dry. Check the meat is tender with a fork, then leave to rest for half an hour, so that when cut into slices it will not break up. Serve with the sauce (which can be puréed if desired).

CALLOS
TRIPE

Ingredients (serves four)

- 1 kg (2 lb) tripe
- 1 beef shank
- 2 pig´s trotters
- 1 calf snout
- 2 onions

- 3 cloves garlic
- Parsley, bay leaf
- Chilli pepper
- 150 g (5 oz) cured ham
  (jamón serrano)

- 100 g (4 oz) chorizo sausage
- White wine
- Paprika, vinegar, salt
- 200 ml (1/3 pint) olive oil

Preparation

Wash the tripe in plenty of cold water, and leave for an hour in water with salt and vinegar, then rinse until the vinegar smell disappears. Cut into even-sized pieces and boil in a pan for seven minutes. Drain and place in cold water, together with a clove of garlic, a chopped onion, parsley, bay leaf and salt for four hours. Drain and put to one side.

Flame the beef shank, the pig's trotters and the snout, in order to remove any hairs. Scrub with a brush and rinse. Simmer for three hours, then remove from the pan and put the resulting gelatine stock to one side.

Chop the shank, trotters and snout, and mix with the cooked tripe.

Chop the onion and chilli and fry. When the onion begins to brown, add the ham and the diced chorizo. Sauté and add a tablespoonful of paprika.

In a separate pan, fry two cloves of garlic and a few sprigs of parsley, crush in a mortar and add to the onion. Pour in a glass of white wine and leave to boil. Place the tripe, shank, trotters and snout in a casserole dish and pour the sauce over the top. Add some of the gelatine stock (enough to ensure a liquid sauce), season with salt and cook on a low heat for another hour.

Serve hot.

CARACOLES EN SALSA
SNAILS IN SAUCE

Ingredients (serves four)

- 600 g (1¹/₄ lb) snails
- 100 g (4 oz) cured ham (*jamón serrano*)
- 250 g (8 oz) pork belly fat (*tocino*)
- 100 g (4 oz) ground almonds
- 1 sweet red pepper (*pimiento choricero*)
- 2 tomatoes
- 1 onion
- 1 clove garlic
- Parsley, Bay leaf
- Chilli
- White wine
- 150 ml (¹/₄ pint) olive oil
- Salt

Preparation

Clean the snails well in plenty of cold water. Leave them to soak for two hours in water, salt and vinegar, rinsing several times, before cooking for 10 minutes. Rinse again several times until the smell of vinegar disappears.

Boil for 10 minutes in water, then rinse again with cold water.

Bring a pan of salted water to the boil and add the snails, together with a few pieces of onion, a clove of garlic, parsley and a bay leaf. Cook for an hour and a half. Drain well and place in an earthenware casserole dish.

Meanwhile, chop the onion and poach in oil. Peel and chop the tomatoes, and soak the pepper to remove the flesh, and add both to the onion when it begins to brown.

Dice the ham and pork fat and sauté in a second frying pan, then add to the tomato sauce. Stir in the almonds, half a glass of wine and a chilli pepper, bring to the boil and pour over the snails.

Cook for half an hour, adding water if necessary.

Serve hot, together with the sauce, in the same dish.

CERDO CON ALCACHOFAS
PORK WITH ARTICHOKES

Ingredients (serves four)

- 750 g (1³/₄ lb) lean pork
- 1 onion
- 2 green peppers
- 3 cloves garlic
- 1 tsp paprika
- 200 g (7 oz) peas
- 4 artichokes
- 2 sprigs parsley
- 1 glass white wine
- 1 kg (2 lb) potatoes
- Saffron
- 1 lemon
- 150 ml (¹/₄ pint) olive oil
- Salt

Preparation

Sauté the vegetables in olive oil: first the chopped peppers and then the onion (in rings) and the garlic (in thin slices). Discard the outer leaves of the artichokes, and spread with lemon to prevent discolouring, then add to the pan when the onion begins to clear, along with the peas.

Chop the meat, add to the vegetables and cook for a couple of minutes before adding the glass of wine and the paprika. Cook on a low heat, adding a glass of hot water after five minutes. Season with salt and a few threads of saffron, then leave to cook for an hour on a low heat.

Twenty minutes before the end, add the peeled chopped potatoes. Check for salt. When the stew is ready, remove from the heat, sprinkle with chopped parsley and serve.

CERDO ESTOFADO CON PATATAS Y COLES DE BRUSELAS
PORK STEW WITH POTATOES AND BRUSSELS SPROUTS

Ingredients (serves four)

- 250 g (9 oz) pork
- 1 kg (2 lb) potatoes
- 300 g (10 oz) Brussels sprouts
- 150 g (5 oz) peas
- 1 red pepper

- 2 tomatoes
- 3 carrots
- 1 onion
- 2 cloves garlic
- 1 tablespoon paprika

- 1 glass white wine
- 150 ml (1/4 pint) olive oil
- Salt

Preparation

Dice the meat, season with salt and fry in plenty of olive oil until brown. Chop the onion, garlic and pepper and add to the meat, and when they are almost done add the peeled chopped tomatoes. Fry for two minutes, add a spoonful of paprika and then the white wine. Cook for a couple of minutes more, then add the peeled diced potatoes, the peas, sliced carrots and Brussels sprouts. Cover with water, add salt and cook on a low heat until the vegetables are tender.

CHULETA DE TERNERA CON SALSA DE MOSTAZA
VEAL CHOPS WITH MUSTARD SAUCE

Ingredients (serves four)

- 4 veal chops
- 1 onion
- 1 glass white wine
- 4 tsp Dijon mustard
- 4 tbsp cream
- $^{1}/_{2}$ tsp thyme
- Ground black pepper
- 125 ml (8 tbsp) olive oil
- Coarse salt

Preparation

Finely chop the onion and brown on a low heat in six or seven tablespoons of oil, then pour in a glass of white wine and cook to reduce the liquid by half. Now add the mustard and cream, stirring with a wooden spoon. Cook for two or three more minutes and season with salt and pepper.

Brush the meat with a little oil and grill or cook in a frying pan, first on a high heat and then lower, for around three minutes each side, seasoning with salt and thyme.

Serve on a platter covered with the mustard sauce, with a side dish of fries.

CODILLOS DE CERDO ESTOFADOS
STEWED PIG'S KNUCKLES

Ingredients (serves four)

- 4 pig's knuckles
- 2 onions
- 1 leek
- 1 carrot

- 1 bay leaf
- 6 cloves garlic
- 1^1/$_2$ glasses white wine
- ^{1}/$_4$ glass brandy

- ^{1}/$_4$ tsp thyme
- 200 ml (^{1}/$_3$ pint) olive oil
- Salt

Preparation

Season the knuckles and brown in olive oil, then remove from the pan and put to one side.

Use the same oil to sauté the onions, leek, carrot and garlic, all finely chopped. Add the thyme and bay leaf.

When the sauté is cooked, return the knuckles to the pan, pour in the white wine and brandy, cover and cook for an hour and a quarter until tender. Add water if the sauce becomes too thick.

CODORNICES CON CHAMPIÑONES
QUAILS WITH MUSHROOMS

Ingredients (serves four)

- 8 quails
- 150 g (5 oz) cured ham
- 200 g (7 oz) mushrooms
- 1¹/₂ onions
- 1¹/₂ glasses white wine
- ¹/₂ tsp thyme
- 3 cloves garlic
- 1 tsp chopped parsley
- 150 ml (¹/₄ pint) olive oil
- Salt

Preparation

Rinse the quails with water and dry with a clean cloth. Season with salt and brown in hot olive oil, then remove and put to one side.

Chop the onion into large pieces and fry in the same oil, then add the sliced mushrooms and diced ham, and sauté for a couple of minutes. Crush the garlic and parsley in a mortar, mix with the white wine and add to the pan, strirring well. Now add the birds, sprinkle with the thyme and cook on a low heat for half an hour before serving.

CONEJO EN PEPITORIA
RABBIT FRICASSEE

Ingredients (serves four)

- 1 rabbit
- 100 g (3^1/$_2$ oz) raw peeled almonds
- 1 onion
- 2 cloves garlic
- 2 hardboiled egg yolks
- Saffron
- 1 glass white wine
- ^{1}/$_2$ glass chicken (or similar) stock
- Ground white pepper
- 150 ml (^{1}/$_4$ pint) olive oil
- Salt

Preparation

Clean the rabbit with cold water and dry with a clean cloth. Cut into pieces and season with salt and pepper.

Fry the rabbit pieces in hot olive oil until brown on all sides, then remove and place in a casserole dish.

Chop the garlic and fry in the same oil. Before it browns add a glass of white wine and a few threads of saffron, previously toasted in a dry hot frying pan. Boil for two minutes, then pour over the meat and cook on a low heat for around forty minutes until tender.

Meanwhile, crush the almonds in a mortar along with the egg yolks, stir in the stock and add to the rabbit. Check for salt and stir well with a wooden spoon for ten more minutes before serving.

CONEJO ESTOFADO
RABBIT STEW

Ingredients (serves four)

- 1 rabbit, weighing 1$^1/_2$ kg (3$^1/_2$ lb)
- 2 onions
- 2 tomatoes
- 4 cloves garlic
- 1 glass brandy

- 1 glass white wine
- 1 kg (2 lb) potatoes
- 1 leek
- 1 bay leaf
- $^1/_2$ tsp thyme

- Ground white pepper
- 150 ml ($^1/_4$ pint) olive oil
- Salt

Preparation

Chop the rabbit into pieces and brown in olive oil, then remove from the pan and put to one side.

Use the same oil to sauté the chopped onion, garlic and leek. After three minutes add the peeled chopped tomatoes and cook for two more minutes. After this time, add the meat to the pan, along with the bay leaf and the thyme. Season with salt and pepper and pour in the brandy, white wine and half a glass of water. Cook on a low heat for around an hour.

While the rabbit is cooking, peel and dice the potatoes, then add to the stew twenty minutes before the meat is ready. Check for salt and serve.

CORDERO LECHAL GUISADO
SUCKLING LAMB STEW

Ingredients (serves four)

- 1¹/₂ kg (3¹/₂ lb) young lamb
- 1 onion
- 4 cloves garlic
- 1 red pepper
- 2 lemons
- 500 ml (I pint) dry white wine
- 150 ml (¹/₄ pint) olive oil
- Salt

Preparation

The night before, cut the meat up and dress with salt, the juice of the two lemons, a squirt of olive oil and another of white wine.

The next day, brown the meat in a pan with olive oil. Add the onion and garlic and fry gently. Now add the white wine and cook for around three quarters of an hour, until the lamb is tender. The stew is finished when the meat comes easily off the bone. Blend the sauce before serving.

FIAMBRE DE PAVO
TURKEY LUNCHMEAT

Ingredients (serves four)

- 750 g (1 $^3/_4$ lb) turkey breast
- 2 leeks
- 1 onion
- 1 small tin red bell peppers
- $^1/_2$ courgette
- 75 g (3 oz) cured ham slices
- 2 eggs
- $^1/_2$ tsp oregano
- 2 cloves garlic
- Ground white pepper
- 150 ml ($^1/_4$ pint) olive oil
- Salt

Preparation

Cut the turkey breast open in the manner of a book and rub with the garlic, parsley and oregano, crushed in a mortar.

Roughly chop the vegetables and sauté in a third of the olive oil. When they begin to soften add the ham, cut into thick strips, fry lightly then add the beaten eggs, allowing them to set like an omelette.

Place the omelette over the turkey breast, roll it up and tie with twine.

Brown the turkey roll in the rest of the (very hot) oil and place in the oven pre-heated to 170º C (340º F) for half an hour.

Serve in slices, hot or cold.

HÍGADO DE TERNERA GUISADO
STEWED CALF'S LIVER

Ingredients (serves four)

- 750 g (1 3/4 lb) calf's liver
- 1/2 glass white wine
- 4 cloves garlic
- 1 tbsp flour
- 1/4 glass meat stock
- 1/2 tsp chopped parsley
- 150 ml (1/4 pint) olive oil
- Salt

Preparation

Chop the liver into pieces and rub with salt and chopped garlic.

Sauté the liver in hot olive oil for five minutes, then remove from the pan and put to one side.

In the same oil, dissolve a spoonful of flour and stir in the white wine, stock and chopped parsley. Bring to the boil and simmer for five minutes, stirring with a wooden spoon. Check for salt.

Return the liver to the pan, covering it entirely with the sauce, and cook for three more minutes.

Serve with chips or boiled rice.

LACÓN DE JABALÍ ASADO
ROAST SHOULDER OF WILD BOAR

Ingredients (serves four)

- 1 1/2 kg (3 lb) wild boar shoulder
- 4 cloves garlic
- 1 bay leaf
- 1 glass white wine
- 1/2 tsp thyme
- 1/2 lemon
- 200 ml (1/3 pint) olive oil
- Salt

Preparation

Place the meat in a bowl along with the crushed garlic, bay leaf, thyme, a glass of white wine and salt. Cover the meat with water, then place in the fridge for two days.

After this time, drain the meat and place in an ovenproof dish.

Heat the olive oil in a frying pan, and when it starts to smoke add the meat to form a crust and seal in the moisture.

Place in the oven, preheated to 200° C (390° C), basting with the stock from the marinade and the juice of half a lemon. Repeat this process every five minutes while roasting. Roasting time will depend on the size and age of the animal. The meat is ready when it easily pricked with a skewer. Serve with fries and roast peppers.

LENGUA DE TERNERA ESTOFADA
STEWED CALF'S TONGUE

Ingredients (serves four)

- 1 calf's tongue, 1 kg (2 lb)
- 1 green pepper
- 2 onions
- 2 tomatoes

- 4 cloves garlic
- 1 bay leaf
- 1 tbsp paprika
- 4 sprigs parsley

- 2 glasses white wine
- 150 ml (1/4 pint) olive oil
- Salt

Preparation

Blanch the tongue in boiling water in order to remove the skin. Now rub with salt and crushed garlic and leave to sit for a couple of hours.

Brown the tongue in a casserole dish with plenty of very hot oil, turning the tongue several times. Chop the onion and pepper and add to the pan, then three or four minutes later add the peeled chopped tomato, the bay leaf and a spoonful of paprika. Sauté for three more minutes.

Crush two cloves of garlic and the parsley in a mortar, mix with two glasses of wine and pour this mixture into the casserole dish and cook on a low heat for two hours, until the tongue is tender (check by skewering it with a needle).

The sauce can be puréed, if desired. Serve the tongue cut into slices with the sauce over the top.

LOMO DE TERNERA ASADO
ROAST BEEF

Ingredients (serves four)

- 600 g (1 1/4 lb) beef loin
- 1 l (1 3/4 pints) meat stock
- 1/2 l (16 fl oz) dry white wine
- 2 tsp corn flour
- 150 ml (1/4 pint) olive oil
- Salt

Preparation

Brush the meat with olive oil and leave to sit for an hour, then season with a little salt before browning evenly all over in very hot olive oil. Place the meat on a baking tray, add the white wine and meat stock, and place in a preheated oven at 200° C (390° F), turning regularly and basting with the juices until roasted.

The sauce can be thickened, if desired, with a little corn flour diluted in cold water, checking the sauce for salt.

Finally leave the meat to sit in the oven (switched off) for fifteen minutes before carving into thin slices.

MANITAS DE CERDO ESTOFADAS
STEWED PIG'S TROTTERS

Ingredients (serves four)

- 4 pig's trotters
- 2 onions
- 1 clove garlic
- Paprika

- White wine
- Black peppercorns
- Bay leaf
- Chilli pepper

- Parsley
- 150 ml ($^1/_4$ pint) olive oil
- Salt

Preparation

Use front trotters, as they have more meat. Most butchers sell them ready cleaned and split in two. Tie them with string so they keep their shape during the cooking.

In a pan with plenty of salted water, cook the trotters together with a piece of onion, a clove of garlic, a bay leaf and a few peppercorns. Simmer on a low heat for 3 hours, then remove the trotters from the pan and put the stock to one side.

Finely chop an onion and gently sauté in a casserole dish with a little oil. Crush the garlic and parsley in a mortar, mix with half a glass of white wine, and add to the onion when it begins to brown. Add a teaspoonful of paprika and a bay leaf, and then add the trotters. Cover and cook for an hour, adding stock if the sauce becomes too dry. Add a chilli pepper for a spicier flavour.

Serve hot.

MUSLOS DE POLLO AL CAVA
CHICKEN LEGS WITH CAVA

Ingredients (serves four)

- 4 whole chicken legs
- 1 onion
- 4 cloves garlic
- 1 bay leaf

- 1 carrot
- Black peppercorns
- 1/2 tsp oregano
- 1/4 glass vinegar

- 1/2 glass poultry stock
- 1 glass Cava sparkling wine
- 150 ml (1/4 pint) olive oil
- Salt

Preparation

Brown the chicken legs in olive oil, remove from the frying pan and put to one side.

Use the same oil to sauté the onion chopped into rings, the chopped carrot and the cloves of garlic sliced into four. Add the oregano, ten to twelve peppercorns and the bay leaf, stirring gently to mix with the vegetables.

Pour in the Cava, the vinegar and the stock, bring to the boil and add the chicken pieces. Season and leave to cook on a low heat for around forty minutes.

PALETILLA DE CORDERO LECHAL AL HORNO
ROAST SHOULDER OF SUCKLING LAMB

Ingredients (serves four)

- 4 suckling lamb shoulders
- 1 l (1 3/4 pints) dry white wine
- 2 lemons
- 4 cloves garlic
- 200 ml (1/3 pint) olive oil
- Salt

Preparation

Dress the meat with salt and crushed garlic, and leave to sit for an hour.

Preheat the oven to 250° C (480° F) and place the lamb shoulders on a baking tray.

Heat the olive oil in a frying pan until it begins to smoke, then pour over the meat along with the white wine, the juice of the two lemons and two glasses of water.

Place the tray in the oven and roast for an hour, turning and basting the meat several times to prevent it drying out (add more water if necessary).

PAVO EN ENSALADA AL VINAGRE DE ARÁNDANOS
TURKEY SALAD WITH CRANBERRY VINEGAR

Ingredients (serves four)

- 400 g (14 oz) turkey leg
- 100 g (3^1/$_2$ oz) cranberry jam
- 1 lettuce
- Sherry vinegar

- Ground white pepper
- 50 ml (3 tbsp) olive oil
- Salt

Preparation

Prepare the vinegar the day before: mix four parts olive oil to one part vinegar; add the jam, salt and pepper, and mix well. Leave to sit for at least a day.

Spread the turkey leg with salt, pepper and olive oil, and grill on a hotplate or in the oven. Cut into strips when fully cooked.

Wash the lettuce and cut into strips (julienne), place on a dish and arrange the turkey over the top. Dress with the vinegar and serve warm.

PERDICES CON COLES
PARTRIDGES WITH BRUSSELS SPROUTS

Ingredients (serves four)

- 2 partridges
- 600 g Brussels sprouts
- 150 g bacon
- 2 carrots
- 1 1/2 onions
- 5 cloves garlic
- 1 glass sherry
- 1 bay leaf
- 150 ml (1/4 pint) olive oil
- Salt

Preparation

Wash the Brussels sprouts and cook in boiling salted water for fifteen minutes, then drain and put to one side.

Season the partridges with salt, then brown in olive oil on all sides, remove from the pan and put to one side.

Chop the onion, slice the carrot and fry in the same oil, then add the bacon, chopped into even pieces, followed by the garlic, crushed in a mortar and mixed with the sherry.

Return the birds to the pan, add the bay lead and cook for around three quarters of an hour, adding a little water if the sauce becomes too thick.

Sauté the sprout in a little olive oil with two cloves of garlic, and arrange on a platter with the partridges in the middle. Pour the sauce from the birds over the top and serve hot.

PERDIZ CON LOMBARDA Y SALSA DE MANZANAS
PARTRIDGE WITH RED CABBAGE AND APPLE SAUCE

Ingredients (serves four)

- 2 partridges
- 700 g (1^1/$_2$ lb) red cabbage
- 200 g (7 oz) cured ham
- 2 onions
- 2 apples

- 4 cloves garlic
- 3 glasses white wine
- 2 tbsp sugar
- ^{1}/$_2$ tsp oregano
- 1 bay leaf

- Ground black pepper
- 150 ml (^{1}/$_4$ pint) olive oil
- Salt

Preparation

Wash the cabbage and chop into julienne, then cook in salted water for fifteen minutes before draining and putting to one side.

Crush the garlic in a mortar, rub over the birds and leave to sit for an hour.

Brown the partridges on all sides in hot olive oil, then remove from the pan and put to one side.

Finely chop the onion and fry in the same oil, then add the ham, cut into 2 cm/1 inch pieces, and sauté gently.

Now add the birds, along with the bay leaf, oregano and two glasses of white wine. Cook for around three quarters of an hour, until the meat is tender.

Prepare the sauce by peeling the apples and slicing into four, removing the centre area and filleting the resulting pieces. Cook on a low heat with a glass of white wine and two tablespoons of sugar for fifteen minutes, then blend with a food mixer.

Place the partridges on a platter. Mix the onion sauce thoroughly with the cabbage, and arrange this around the birds. Serve with the apple sauce on the side.

PIERNA DE CABRITO CON VERDURAS
LEG OF KID WITH VEGETABLES

Ingredients (serves four)

- 2 kid legs, 1¹/₄ kg (2³/₄ lb) each
- 4 tomatoes
- 2 onions
- ³/₄ kg (1¹/₂ lb) potatoes
- 4 cloves garlic
- 1 glass white wine
- 1 tsp thyme
- 350 ml (²/₃ pint) olive oil
- Salt

Preparation

Place the legs on a baking tray, sprinkle with salt and thyme, and drizzle with 200 ml (13 tbsp) of very hot olive oil. Place in the oven, preheated to 250° C (480° F) for fifteen minutes.

Meanwhile, peel and roughly chop the tomatoes, chop the garlic cloves in half, and slice the onion into thick rings. Place the vegetables around the meat and leave to cook for another quarter of an hour.

Cut the potatoes into slices and fry gently with the rest of the olive oil for around four minutes, then place among the other vegetables, pour over a glass of white wine and leave to cook for another fifteen minutes before serving.

POLLO AL AJILLO
CHICKEN IN GARLIC

Ingredients (serves four)

- 1 chicken
- 6 cloves garlic
- Olive oil
- Brandy
- Salt

Preparation

Burn off the remains of any feathers, wash the chicken, dry well and cut into small pieces.

Thinly slice the garlic and use to rub the chicken pieces, together with a little brandy. Leave to stand for an hour, then remove the garlic pieces and put to one side.

Season the chicken and fry in batches in hot oil until golden brown.

Use part of the same oil to fry the garlic left over from marinating the meat, and pour over the chicken.

Serve straight away, sprinkled with chopped parsley (optional).

POLLO CON SETAS
CHICKEN WITH MUSHROOMS

Ingredients (serves four)

- 1 chicken weighing 2 kg (4 1/2 lb)
- 400 g (14 oz) wild (pleurotus eryngii) or domestic mushrooms
- 1 glass red wine
- 1 glass brandy
- 2 leeks
- 1 onion
- 2 carrots
- 2 cloves garlic
- 1 tomato
- Ground white pepper
- 200 ml (1/3 pint) olive oil
- Salt

Preparation

Cut the chicken into pieces and season with salt and pepper.

Brown the chicken in three quarters of the oil, which must be very hot. Use the same oil to fry the chopped onion, leek, carrot and garlic, as well as the peeled chopped tomato. When this sauté is soft add the brandy and flambé the mixture, then add the red wine. Cook for thirty minutes on a low heat.

While the chicken is cooking, clean and chop the mushrooms, and add them to the chicken around seven minutes before the end of the cooking time.

RABO DE TERNERA AL VINO TINTO
CALF'S TAIL IN RED WINE

Ingredients (serves four)

- 1¹/₂ kg (3 lb) calf's tail
- ¹/₂ glass red wine
- 2 onions
- 50 g (2 oz) flour

- 1 leek
- 1 carrot
- 3 cloves garlic
- ¹/₄ tsp thyme

- 1 glass brandy
- 1 glass meat stock
- 200 ml (¹/₃ pint) olive oil
- Salt

Preparation

Cut the tail into pieces at the joints, season and marinate for 24 hours with the red wine, the roughly chopped vegetables, the cloves of garlic (whole) and the thyme.

After this time, coat the tail pieces in flour and fry in olive oil. Add the vegetables and garlic and sauté on a lower heat until they are soft. Now add the brandy and flambé, and then pour in the wine from the marinade, and leave to cook for an hour on a low heat. Add a little stock as the wine evaporates.

Once the tail is cooked, place in a casserole dish and blend the sauce.

RIÑONES AL JEREZ
KIDNEYS IN SHERRY

Ingredients (serves four)

- 500 g (1 lb) kidneys
  (pig or calf)
- 1 onion
- 2 cloves garlic
- Flour

- Parsley
- Dry sherry
- Lemon or vinegar
- 100 ml (7 tbsp) olive oil
- Salt

Preparation

Clean the kidneys, cut into slices and remove any skin and fat. Sprinkle with lemon juice or vinegar and put to one side for half an hour.

Place the kidneys in a sieve or metal colander and scald by lowering into a pan with boiling water for half a minute. Remove and leave to dry.

Crush the garlic in a mortar, add half a glass of sherry and use the mixture to rub the kidneys. Leave to stand for an hour and a half.

Finely chop the onion and a few sprigs of parsley and fry in hot oil. Add the kidneys when the onion begins to brown. Season and cook on a high heat for 5 minutes. Add another half glass of sherry and a tablespoonful of flour. Stir well and cook on a low heat for a further 5 minutes.

Serve piping hot.

ROLLO DE CARNE PICADA
MINCED BEEF ROLL

Ingredients (serves four)

- 600 g (1 1/4 lb) minced beef
- 50 g (2 oz) stale bread
- 1/2 glass milk
- 2 cloves garlic

- 1/2 tsp chopped parsley
- 1 egg
- 50 g (2 oz) breadcrumbs
- 1 glass white wine

- 1/2 glass brandy
- 150 ml (1/4 pint) olive oil
- Salt

Preparation

Place the mince, parsley, crushed garlic, stale bread (soaked in milk then drained), egg and salt in a deep bowl. Mix with your hands to form a large roll.

Coat in the breadcrumbs then brown on all sides in hot olive oil.

Remove from the pan and place on a baking tray. Add the white wine, brandy and half a glass of water. Place in the oven preheated to 180° C (360° F) and roast for an hour, basting several times with the liquid (add more water if necessary).

Serve arranged in slices.

SOLOMILLO DE CERDO AL JEREZ
PORK TENDERLOIN WITH SHERRY

Ingredients (serves four)

- 1 kg (2 lb) pork tenderloin
- 100 g (3^1/$_2$ oz) slices cured ham
- 1 glass sherry
- 8 button onions
- ^{1}/$_4$ tsp thyme
- ^{1}/$_2$ glass meat stock
- 100 ml (7 tbsp) olive oil
- Salt

Preparation

Cut the ham into strips and wrap around the pork. Season with salt and thyme, then tie up with twine to keep its shape, and leave to sit for two hours.

After this time, brown in a casserole dish with olive oil, then remove and place in an ovenproof dish. Drizzle with the oil used to brown the meat, along with the sherry and meat stock. Place in the oven, preheated to 200° C (390° F), for around forty minutes, occasionally basting the meat with the sauce.

Meanwhile, peel the onions and place them around the meat halfway through the cooking time, spooning the sauce over them.

When cooked, remove from the oven and discard the twine. Cut into slices, arrange the onions around the side and cover with the sauce. Can be served with mashed potato or fries.

SOLOMILLO HOJALDRADO
TENDERLOIN IN PASTRY

Ingredients (serves four)

- 1 kg (2 lb) tenderloin, either veal or pork
- 1 sheet pre-cooked pastry
- 250 g (9 oz) bacon rashers
- 1 egg
- 100 ml (7 tbsp) olive oil
- Salt

Preparation

Season the tenderloin and brown in hot olive oil. Remove and wrap completely in the bacon. Then wrap in the pastry, trimming off the edges.

Decorate the surface with various shapes by using the pastry trimmings.

Brush the top of the pastry with the beaten egg to produce a shine after baking.

Place the meat on an ovenproof tray and place in the oven, preheated to 170º C (340º F), for fifteen minutes until the pastry is golden brown.

Can be served with mushrooms sautéed in olive oil.

TERNERA A LA JARDINERA
BEEF AND VEGETABLE STEW

Ingredients (serves four)

- 750 g (1³/₄ lb) beef
- 250 g (9 oz) peas
- 150 g (5 oz) mushrooms
- 3 carrots
- 2 tomatoes

- 1 green pepper
- 1 tin red bell peppers
- 4 potatoes
- 1 onion
- 3 cloves garlic

- 4 sprigs parsley
- 2 glasses white wine
- 200 ml (¹/₃ pint) olive oil
- Salt

Preparation

Cut the meat into large pieces and rub with two cloves of garlic crushed in a mortar, then leave to sit for at least half an hour.

Meanwhile, thinly slice the carrots, chop the onion and green pepper, and peel and chop the tomatoes.

Cover the bottom of a casserole dish with olive oil and place on the heat. Season the meat, and when the oil is hot add to the casserole to brown. Then add the carrots, onion and pepper, sauté lightly and add the tomatoes, sliced mushrooms and peas.

Crush a clove of garlic and the parsley in mortar, mix with the white wine and add to the meat. Cook for around an hour until the meat is tender.

Serve with fried potato slices and red pepper cut into strips.

TERNERA AL AJILLO CON TOMATE
BEEF WITH GARLIC AND TOMATO

Ingredients (serves four)

- 750 g (1$^3/_4$ lb) beef shank
- 8 cloves garlic
- 500 g (1 lb) tomatoes

- 1 slice fried bread
- $^1/_4$ glass white wine
- 1 glass meat stock

- $^1/_4$ tsp oregano
- 150 ml ($^1/_4$ pint) olive oil
- Salt

Preparation

Cut the meat into large pieces, rub with two cloves of chopped garlic and leave to sit for half an hour.

Meanwhile, sauté the peeled chopped tomatoes in a third of the oil and the oregano, then put to one side.

Season the meat with salt and brown in the rest of the olive oil. Crush the fried bread in a mortar along with two cloves of garlic, and mix with the white wine. Add this mixture to the meat, then add the tomatoes, the remaining garlic cloves (whole) and the meat stock. Cook on a low heat for around an hour, check for salt and remove the whole garlic cloves when ready to serve.

TERNERA ESTOFADA
STEWED BEEF

Ingredients (serves four)

- 1 kg (2 lb) beef shank
- $1/2$ green pepper
- $1/2$ red pepper
- 1 onion
- 2 cloves garlic
- 2 carrots
- $1/2$ glass white wine
- $1/2$ glass brandy
- 150 ml ($1/4$ pint) olive oil
- Salt

Preparation

Cut the beef into large pieces, season and fry in olive oil, without the meat browning. Remove from the pan and put to one side.

Use the same oil to gently fry the onion, peppers, garlic and carrot, all chopped. Add the meat, along with the wine and brandy, and leave to cook on a low heat for around an hour and a half, until the beef is tender.

The sauce can be blended or served as is.

TERNERA GUISADA CON SALSA DE ALMENDRAS
STEWED BEEF WITH ALMOND SAUCE

Ingredients (serves four)

- 750 g (1³/₄ lb) beef shank
- 50 g (2 oz) roasted almonds
- ¹/₂ glass white wine
- 6 cloves garlic

- 1 glass meat stock
- 1 slice fried bread
- 1 onion
- Ground pepper

- 100 ml (7 tbsp) olive oil
- Salt

Preparation

Cut the beef into pieces and rub with salt and two cloves of crushed garlic, and leave to sit for half an hour.

Brown the meat in the olive oil (it should be very hot), remove from the pan and put to one side.

Use the same oil to sauté the onion, a sprig of parsley and the remaining cloves of garlic, all crushed together in a mortar. When the onion is cooked, add the white wine and boil for two minutes, then return the meat to the pan.

Crush the fried bread and the almonds in a mortar to form a paste. Dilute with a glass of stock and add to the meat. Cook on a low heat for around an hour, seasoning with salt and pepper to taste. Finally, blend the sauce and serve poured over the beef.

TIMBAL DE POLLO
CHICKEN PIE

Ingredients (serves four)

For the dough:
- 1 glass white wine
- 1 glass olive oil
- 700 g (1¹/₂ lb) flour
- Salt

For the filling:
- 1 chicken, in pieces
- ¹/₂ onion
- 1 green pepper
- 50g (2 oz) cured ham

- 1 egg
- 1 glass white wine
- 150 ml (¹/₄ pint) olive oil
- Salt

Preparation

For the dough: mix the olive oil, wine and salt, beating until milky, then gradually add the flour, stirring well until the dough is formed. Leave to sit for half an hour in a cool place.

For the filling: Season the chicken with salt and fry in olive oil until brown on all sides, then remove from the pan and put to one side.

Chop the pepper and onion and fry in the same oil. When they are soft, add the diced ham and sauté gently. Now return the chicken to the pan, pour in the white wine and cook for half an hour, the remove from the heat and leave to cool. Pick the meat off the bones, strain the sauce to remove excess fat and mix the two to form the stuffing.

Spread the dough out with a rolling pin to a thickness of around 1 cm (¹/₂ inch). Use half of it to line an ovenproof dish, previously greased with oil and sprinkled with flour, and with the pastry hanging over the edge slightly. Now add the filling, spreading it out evenly. Cover with the other half of the pastry and close the edges by pressing down with your fingers. Adorn the surface with any dough left over in the form of patterns and shapes, and brush with egg to provide a shine. Place in the oven, preheated to 180° C (360° F) for half an hour until the pastry is cooked.

VENADO EN SALSA DE CABRALES
VENISON WITH CABRALES CHEESE SAUCE

Ingredients (serves four)

- 4 venison fillets, 250 g (9 oz) each
- 4 slices cured ham
- 4 slices cheese
- 1 egg

- 200 g (7 oz) bread crumbs
- 200 g (7 oz) mushrooms
- 250 g (9 oz) Cabrales cheese
- 1 glass white wine
- 150 ml ($1/4$ pint) cream

- 2 cloves garlic
- 250 ml ($1/2$ pint) olive oil
- Salt

Preparation

Lightly season the fillets with salt. Over each one place a slice of ham and then a slice of cheese, then close each one in the manner of a book. Dip in egg and coat in breadcrumbs, and fry in 200 ml ($1/3$ pint) of olive oil on both sides until brown. Remove from the oil and place in an ovenproof dish.

Finely chop the garlic and slice the mushrooms. Heat 50 ml (3 tbsp) of olive oil in another pan and fry the garlic, then add the mushrooms and sauté before adding the white wine. Simmer for a couple of minutes then pour over the fillets.

Place in the oven, preheated to 200º C (390º F) for seven or eight minutes, basting the meat with the sauce two or three times.

Meanwhile, prepare the Cabrales sauce. Lightly grease a frying pan with olive oil and melt the cheese along with the cream, then leave to reduce for a couple of minutes. Blend if preferred for a creamier finish, then serve by pouring the hot sauce over the venison.

INDEX

EL ORO VIRGEN DEL OLIVO . . . . **1** THE VIRGIN GOLD OF THE OLIVE TREE

SOUPS AND CREAMS

VEGETABLES AND PULSES

EGGS AND MUSHROOMS

RICE AND PASTA

FISH AND SEAFOOD

MEAT, FOWL AND GAME

© EDARA EDICIONES, S.L.
CÓRDOBA - Spain

I.S.B.N.: 84-95332-25-6
Depósito Legal: CO. 898-2004
Printed in Spain

A collective work conceived, designed and created by
the Editorial Management of Edara Ediciones, S.L.

Editorial team

Management: ANTONIO ARREBOLA

Text "The Virgin Gold of the Olive Tree": MANUEL PIEDRAHITA,
with photographs by ELEUTERIO ALFÉREZ

Recipes and styling: NATALIA LOZANO,
with photographs by MARCOS MORILLA

Layout: TERESA MÁRQUEZ

Translation: MARTIN PHILLIPS, Babel Córdoba

Engraving and drawings:
by kind permission of PIERALISI ESPAÑA, S.A.